If You're a Christian and Everyone Likes You...

Something's Wrong

Sara Dormon

DEDICATION

To my husband, Bill Dormon, my tether and soft place to land.
Thank you for being the man of God I needed
at a time when I needed Him most.

"God's commandments are as confining and restrictive to a Christian as wings are to an eagle."

If You're a Christian and Everyone Likes You...

Something's Wrong

"Taking the words of Jesus seriously."

FOREWORD

Sara Dormon's ability to speak God's truth came into my life like a spring storm, full of force but bringing the promise of beauty and renewed life.

I gave my heart to Christ in my late 20's, but like every human being I've ever met, there are huge areas of sin that I struggle with. I was struggling, ok not really struggling more like surrendering to sin, when my friend Sara confronted me in love..."how's that working for you"? she asked. Not with a judgmental tone, not sarcastically, she looked in my eyes and looked into my heart. I could tell by the look on her face that she understood my struggle and my pain, I fought back tears, and she enveloped me in her arms.

Sara is like that, bold with her words and quick with her love and grace. She listened to me spill my heart over a relationship that was stealing my joy and impeding my walk with God, and she said "you know what you must do, I am here to pray for you until you're ready to submit and obey."

When I am out of step with God it is never because He's changed his pace or His course, it's always because I've stepped away, or simply sat down. Submitting and obeying is so easy for me in many areas, I don't struggle with cheating on my taxes or paying my tithes. Never felt tempted to steal money from the offering plate or from anyone in business deals...I don't battle alcoholism, never had to go to rehab for cocaine or heroin... Many areas of God's word seem simple to obey, but that is because we all have different areas of struggle and temptation. The fact that some areas of obedience come easy to me but are tough for others doesn't make me a spiritual Saint. Because other areas that God calls me to walk in obedience were seemingly IMPOSSIBLE!! "Really God? You want me to end this relationship that means everything to me just because he is technically still married"!?! I know what God's word says about sexual sin, but daily I struggled with obedience, until finally I tossed in the towel and gave in to my passions. Many of my friends turned a blind eye to my situation, not Sara.

Each day God shines His love in our life through His word and His Holy Spirit. Each day we can respond with a resounding "yes"! Or a more defiant "not today, can't do that"...either way, God's love never waivers. But we are cheating ourselves out of sweet blessings when we choose, like stubborn toddlers, to set our face, cross our arms and say "no" to God.

In this book Sara challenges us to be wild, bold, extravagant in our love for the Lord! To listen, submit and let God mold us into His likeness. She encourages us to seek His Holiness, to purge our hearts and lives from the sins that separate us from His glory. In doing so we are able to clearly hear his nudging and respond to His calling in our lives. So be bold! Be wildly in love with Christ!

Delilah - Radio Personality, Author, Artist, Mother to 13
www.delilah.com

CONTENTS

INTRODUCTION

"Woe to you when all men speak well of you."
Luke 6:26

In the United States we have adopted, for the most part, a barely recognizable form of Christianity that almost completely ignores the teachings given in the Bible by the man we say we want to follow and be like: Jesus. We have allowed the secular humanists to dictate what we see on television, hear on radio, and read in the newspaper. And, God help us if we take a stand for what we believe, our principals, or our values. If we say marriage is meant to be between a man and a woman, we are being intolerant and judgmental. If we say sex is to be confined to marriage, we are being unrealistic and narrow. If we say abortion is wrong, well, we're told our laws say it is legal, and we can't take care of millions of unwanted children. Divorce, addiction, abuse, infidelity, depression, abortion, pornography, and a general lack of accountability have all have made their home in the Christian community.

We say, as Christians, we want to be held accountable,

1

but when someone actually does it, all bets are off. Worse yet, we see and hear things we know are clearly out of bounds and clearly against biblical teaching and God's will, but do we say anything? Of course not. We don't want to hurt anyone's feelings or rock anyone's boat. Forget about rocking the boat—we need to turn it over in deep water, without life jackets, in stormy seas until we get everyone's attention. Sound a little harsh? Indeed, it is, but if we, as Christians, do not get the message that we are called to obedience and to be vocal followers of Jesus Christ, then we are in more trouble than most of us think.

Would anyone be able to pick you out of the crowd at your place of work or in your neighborhood and identify you as a Christian? "I know they are Christians." "I know they are followers of Jesus." How would they know? What makes you look, act, think, or speak differently than those with whom you work or live? I am sorry to say that most of the Christians I know, myself included, blend in rather well into the landscape of our world that is in a state of serious moral, spiritual, physical, and emotional decay.

I have just celebrated the forty-eighth anniversary of my acceptance of Jesus Christ as my Lord and Savior. As I sat at a dinner that night, listening to Ben Haden, an evangelist, speak, he made a comment that forever changed my life. "The greatest form of hate or contempt is indifference. Ask any woman." It was at that point that I realized that I wasn't for God, or against Him; I was indifferent.

In Matthew 5:37 God says, "Simply let your 'yes' be 'yes' and your 'no' be 'no'; anything beyond this comes from the evil one." And, in Revelation 3:15, God says, "I know your deeds, that you are neither hot nor cold—I am about to spit you out of my mouth."

On my walk, I have taken more than one detour from the Jesus that I said yes to, but in spite of those, my stubbornness, my self-righteous arrogance, and a litany of other shortcomings, I have learned one very important lesson. If God doesn't seem as close to me as He once was, it is I who have moved and not Him.

A good friend, with the voice of an angel, Damaris Carbaugh, sings one of my favorite songs, "He's Been Faithful." While the entire song brings me to tears, one verse in particular speaks to my heart and captures the journey that I am sure many others share. The verse is:

> When my heart looked away, the many times I could not pray,
> still my God, He was faithful to me.
> The days I spent so selfishly, reaching out for what pleased me,
> even then God was faithful to me.
> Every time I come back to Him,
> He is waiting with open arms.
> And, I see once again, He's been faithful, faithful to me.

This book is about how we, as Christians, have either forgotten, or have never known, what the commandments of Jesus are, and what our lives are supposed to look like to the rest of the world and to God. It is about just a few of those things that tend to pull us off track. Those things that we know to be true, to be God's word, but things we find easier to compromise than to follow. Consider 2 Timothy 3:16–17: "All scripture is God-breathed and is useful for teaching, rebuking, correcting, and training in righteousness, so that the man (and woman) of God may be thoroughly equipped for every good work." In Jeremiah 29:11, God says, "I know the plans I have for you, plans to prosper you and not harm you, plans to give you a hope and a future." This is the most often quoted part of this passage; the rest, however, is equally important. "Then, you will call upon me and come and pray to me and I will listen to you. You will seek me and find me when you seek me with all your heart. I will be found by you and will bring you back from captivity." Notice the six action verbs directed at us, and two to God.

The Christian journey is one of action, one in which we are called to live as Christ lived, to follow in His footsteps, to read and heed His word. It is not meant to be easy, but it is meant to make our lives richer, fuller, and more peaceful, and above all else, pleasing to the Father who sacrificed His Son so that we might have eternal life.

This is not about the Ten Commandments. It is about the many other commandments spread throughout the New Testament that we either ignore or don't realize are not really suggestions, but commands, given to us by the Creator of the universe. It is about those "God-breathed" words from the New Testament that are a call to all those who have accepted Jesus as Lord and Savior. They are just a few of those commandments that we overlook, compromise, or totally ignore. Just as we follow the instructions in the owner's manual of our cars, because it is written by the people who built that car, so, too, should we follow our owner's manual of our lives, the Bible, for it was written by God, who is the creator of all life. And, we know that the Father knows best.

Shortly after I became a Christian, a good friend shared an analogy with me that I have never forgotten and use often. She made a cross with two fingers and said, "The vertical piece represents our relationship with God. It must be strong, deeply rooted, and firm in order to hold the horizontal piece, which represents our relationship with everyone else. And, the crossbar cannot exist without the vertical bar." A simple analogy, and a profound truth.

As Christians living in America we appear to have lost our way. Fear not—which is a commandment stated 366 times in the Bible—the road map and the answers we need to find our way home are still where we left them: in the Bible. This book will help us start the journey back, and will hopefully bring us into a right relationship with the Father. God is waiting with open arms, and Our Father is faithful.

- 1 -

OBEDIENCE

"And this is love: that we walk in obedience to His commandments."
2 John 6

When the idea for this book came to me there was one word I kept hearing, and it was the word "obedience." For some reason, I felt that this word was at the root of many of the problems that we face within the Christian community. I certainly know it is a word that I have personally had a few head-on collisions with over the years. So I decided to look the meaning of the word up in the New Oxford American Dictionary. And, guess what I found?

What Is Obedience?

"Compliance with someone's wishes or orders or acknowledgement of their authority: submission to a law or rule." (NOAD, page 1, 173)

Interestingly, a notation after this definition says, "Children and animals may be expected to obey, but nowadays obedient is seldom used to describe adult human beings without a suggestion that they are allowing someone else to assume too great a degree of authority."

As I sat there looking at these words, I wasn't sure if I wanted to be a pet or a child, and then I realized it didn't really matter as far as my obedience was concerned because it stated that I "may be" expected to obey. Actually, I think cats have it pretty good overall. In any event, seeing these words and this definition in print answered many questions that I, and many others, have had for quite some time. "How on earth did we allow things to get so bad?" This question is not just directed at the world at large; it is directed at those of us who call ourselves Christians, followers of Christ, those of us who pride ourselves on our moral compass, our integrity, our compassion, and our obedience.

Obedience Doesn't Always Feel Good

In an absolutely wonderful book, What Happens When Women Say Yes to God, my friend, Lysa TerKeurst, says, "You may be surprised to discover that radical obedience is not really that radical. It is really biblical obedience—but we have strayed so far from biblical obedience that it now seems radical" (TerKeurst 2007 page 18). To that I say amen! I am not sure if we have strayed, because that would mean we have actually, at one time, embraced biblical obedience, and for whatever reason we have stepped away. Drifted may be more accurate. I don't think

8

anyone wakes up one morning and says, "Okay, enough of this obedience-to-Christ stuff." I think we are deeply affected by outside influences and inside influences and we move away slowly and imperceptibly, until we suddenly see God from a distance we never dreamed possible.

Here's an interesting footnote that, in my opinion, demonstrates how the word "obedience" may be offensive to some. When I called Lysa to ask her permission to use her quote, she told me that the book had been given a new title. Its previous title was Radically Obedient, Radically Blessed. The new title is What Happens When Women Say Yes to God. Now, I admit the essence of the two titles is the same: obedience to God is saying yes, in word or action. She said since the title changed, the book has been selling much better. I guess obedience is hard enough—let's not make it radical. If changing the title will get them to buy the book, I say, go for it. Maybe, we should change the title of the Bible to Handbook for Humans.

There is another book out by Dr. Henry Cloud and Dr. John Townsend entitled It's Not My Fault, which runs the following line on the cover: "Who's to blame? People, circumstances, or DNA?" I have great respect for these two men and have read nearly everything they have written, so please understand that my criticisms refer to the title, not the content of the book. A title is what gets people to pick up the book, and with this title they could have put this cover on the yellow pages and people would buy it. We live in a society where no one is to blame for anything. Why? Well, how much time do you have? Obedience to God or anyone else is just too hard and wouldn't we all like to blame our DNA, mother, husband, and children for the mess our lives have become? I am a recovering alcoholic and drug addict and I have been trying to determine who "forced" that first drink or pill on me...ooops! I did! Yes, I am responsible for my choices. I do believe there are predispositions to certain behaviors, but that does not mean they are predetermined. We should treat sin like an allergy to peanuts; the world has transformed to accommodate children for whom peanuts are harmful. Wouldn't it be nice to transform the world to help one another avoid sin? It can be done, if we want to do it.

In a decidedly anti-Christian and anti-God book, The God Delusion by Richard Dawkins, the author writes about hearing a story as a child that deeply impacted his idea of obedience and religion. A group of soldiers were commanded to march forward and when their leader was distracted by something, they kept marching into an oncoming train, because they were being obedient. Sometime ago, I remember hearing a story of a young man who was walking through the forest with his father, and his father turned around and saw a snake hanging from a tree about to attack his son. He said, "Get down on the ground and crawl to me as fast as you can." The boy obeyed and escaped the snake; the soldiers obeyed and they died. God calls us to be obedient to His word but He does not ask us to leave the brains and common sense He gave us at the door. But, the truth is we do have common sense, though most of us don't trust it.

I have often said if common sense were truly common more people would have it. However, we do have it. Again, the problem is that we don't trust it

Obedience Requires Knowing God's Word

Being obedient to God's word first requires that we know what God's word says. And then, once we know what it says and what God expects of us, we must step forward and actually live out His teachings. Ouch! That is the part of obedience that most of us can't seem to get a firm and lasting grip on. For me, obedience often feels like trying to nail Jello to the wall. Why? We are flawed human beings for whom compromise feels better than actually being obedient to what the world tells us are narrow-minded, moralistic, intolerant views. If there is no call to obedience, then all things become tolerated. Tada! And, that ladies and gentlemen, is the world we know today. As Christians, we tend to tolerate those things we shouldn't and be intolerant of those things we should.

A question central to the issue of obedience is:, do we obey God because we know Him or do we know Him because we obey Him? In 1 John 2:3–6, John says:

"It is only when we obey God's laws that we can be quite sure that we really know Him. The man who claims to know God but does not obey His laws is not only a liar but lives in self-delusion. In practice, the more a man learns to obey God's laws

11

the more truly and fully does he express his love for Him. Obedience is the test of whether we really live "in God" or not. The life of a man who professes to be living in God must bear the stamp of Christ." (Phillips NT)

St. Augustine said, "Wicked men obey from fear; good men from love." Those of us with children would love to think that our children do as we say out of their deep love and respect for us. We want to think that our children wake up every morning thinking: How can I please and obey my parents today? How many ways can I show them I love them? I hope I have time to spend with them in order to know them better so that I can obey and please them more. Most (not all children and all adults) obey when it is either convenient for them or the consequences of disobedience are beyond anything even remotely reasonable, even in their minds. In order for us to be obedient to God's word, it has to become an integral part of our lives. His word must abide in us.

I did a word study one time on the word "abide." Abide means "to accept or act in accordance with a rule, decision, or recommendation." (New Oxford, page 3) What does it mean for the word of God to abide in us? What does it mean for us to abide in Christ? My favorite translation of the New Testament is that of J. B. Phillips. I have a copy that was given to me one month after I accepted the Lord. His translation of I John 2:6 is my favorite explanation of the word "abide." "Obedience is the test of whether we really live 'in God' (that is, abide) or not." There is that pesky word again: "obedience."

Being Obedient Is Hard

We have all heard that people are basically good. My response to this claim is always skeptical. If this were, in fact, true, then who taught them how to lie, cheat, steal, and be mean and cruel with little or no regard for another person's feelings? I don't know about you, but these "basically good" qualities came quite naturally to me, and often still do. I live as if I really don't want to be obedient to God. Jesus said, "If you love me you will obey my commandments." Of course, I love Him, as many do. The problem comes in translating that love into living our lives bearing the stamp of Christ.

Why is being obedient to what God teaches us so difficult? We know He loves us more than we ever dreamed possible. We know He has the power and desire to forgive our sins. We know He is slow to anger, compassionate, and wants what is best for us more than we want it for ourselves. Aha! There is the answer. He wants what is best for us. Now if we are honest with ourselves most of us don't even know what is best for us. We know what we want and we know when we want it—now. That's about it. God knew what was best for Adam and Eve, but no, did they listen? One parent, two children...chaos! And, of course, this was the beginning of the blame game. Why would we think we would be any better? Adam and Eve really did live in the Garden of Eden; we just pretend to. Someone once said if sin doesn't feel good you haven't found the right one yet. Laughable on one level and very sad on another. It is like medicine—if it is good for us it will taste bad. There is great freedom that comes with obedience. It is our responsibility to be obedient and the outcome of our obedience is God's job. I repeat: that's God's job, not ours.

The book of James is my favorite of the Bible, and I have often thought that if James and I had lived at the same time we would have been good friends. James was the brother of Jesus and tended to be direct in his words. But, the words he spoke were not his, but the words of his brother Jesus. The way he describes the life we should live is the life Jesus did live. On the surface it may appear to be a moralistic monologue, but in reality he is telling us that to have the life we want and the life God wants for us there are certain things we are expected to do. In James 1:22 he says, "Do not merely listen to the word, and so deceive yourselves. Do what it says." Obedience does not always look good to others or feel good to us, but it is what Jesus requires of us.

I believe, as Christians, we have a tendency to compromise our belief system. We do this in order to not only give others the benefit of the doubt, but in the sincere and earnest hope that they will give us the same. Our willingness and desire to be obedient to the teachings of Jesus is, I believe, at the heart of our entire faith walk. There is no twelve-step program to learn how to deal with our disobedience addiction. It just is what it is. As Paul said in Romans 2:13, "It is not familiarity with the law that justifies a man in the sight of God, but obedience to it." So, we have all heard it all, over and over again. On paper it looks good and in our heads it makes perfect sense. So, exactly where is the disconnection? In what part of our brains, hearts, and souls does our constant and seemingly blatant disobedience reside? It resides in our old sinful, human nature.

"I do not understand what I do. For what I want to do I do not do, but what I hate I do…For I desire to do what is good but I cannot carry it out." (Romans 7:15, 18b)

I recently faced an incident with my son, who, through tears, said, "I knew it was wrong when I did it, but I did it anyway." We may not face situations through tears, although we probably should, but as we walk closer to the Lord our sensitivity to sin increases and the time between sin and confession gets shorter and shorter. Our desire to be obedient increases especially when we see the result of it. But, should we have to see results, or should it just be our desire to be obedient out of our deep love for the Father? "If anyone loves me, he will obey my teachings and we will come to him make our home with him. He who does not love me will not obey me" (John 14:23–24).

I believe, as simple as this sounds, getting this truth to travel from our head to our hearts can be a lifelong journey, one that is often derailed and never easy.

Each and every day we begin our walk with the Lord with a clean slate, a tabula rasa. Each and every day we are given God's grace and mercy, His forgiveness and His joy. We are asked to love Him, obey Him, bear fruit, and live our lives with the stamp of His image upon us. We are to be light in the darkness of a world that is lost. We are to be salty enough to make others thirst for Him. We are to be the hands and feet of Jesus in a hurting and broken world. This begins with our willingness and desire to be obedient to the one who knows us best and loves us most; Jesus Christ, the Son of God.

The Blessings of Obedience

No one is going to tell you that being obedient is easy because it is not. Scripture teaches that. "The heart is deceitful above all things and beyond cure…" (Jeremiah 17:9). This is one of the reasons that the blessings of obedience are so great. In Romans 6:16, it says, "Don't you know that when you offer yourselves to someone to obey as slaves, whether you are slaves to sin, which lead to death, or to obedience, which leads to righteousness?" Now, death or righteousness…okay, I choose righteousness. And, that is just the first of many blessings that come from obedience.

David, one of my favorite scoundrels of the Bible, was referred to as a man after God's own heart and the apple of His eye. As a boy, he spent time alone tending the sheep. David was obedient to God when no one was watching—that is character. And, he was rewarded for his obedience; he became king, although not without a few speed bumps. He trusted His Lord, and killed Goliath when the odds were against him. He was willing to be a fool for Christ. He obeyed God.

Abraham was blessed as were his offspring. "Your descendants will take possession of the cities of their enemies and through your offspring all nations will be blessed, because you have obeyed me" (Genesis 22:17).

There are many examples of the blessings one receives as a result of obedience, but, as Christians, we are called to be obedient because Jesus says, "if you love me you will obey my commandments." To obey the Lord and his teachings is an acknowledgement that we not only love Him, but believe that He knows what is better for us than we do. The blessing is in the knowing that our lives are pleasing to Him. He showed His love for His Father by being obedient, even unto death, which is the blessing we have received from Him, the blessing of eternal life. He will not, however, force His beliefs on us, and if we choose to make our own way, fine, just don't call yourself a Christian. As Andrew Murray said: "Let us care for the obedience, God will care for the blessing. Let my one thought as a Christian be, how I can obey and please my God perfectly."(Andrew Murray, With Christ in the School of Obedience, page 12)

We, as Christians, can easily get discouraged with our seeming lack of progress in the obedience department. But, if you look at it this way it may help. We did not get into this mess overnight, and we aren't going to wake up tomorrow with an uncontrollable desire to be obedient in all things. Each day brings us many decisions, and each one will pull us toward obedience and God or away from Him. The decision is ours each day. It may be two steps forward and one away, but hopefully, you are at least heading in the right direction. And, the blessings will begin the minute we begin to obey.

How Does This Work in My Everyday Life?

Let's just get this out of the way right now. The contents of this book are designed to guide us in our Christian walk, and to know how things should be. So please don't think if you find yourself struggling with obedience, or any of the other issues I will discuss, that you are failing as a Christian. You are not! You're a human being who tries everyday, with God's help, to be the most obedient person and very best version of yourself you can be. And, guess what? We all fail over and over. But, the measure of our success is not how much we fail, but how often we get back up and move on. Even when we fall on our faces we are moving forward.

My belief is that if we aren't willing to be obedient to what we know God demands, then the rest of this book will be of little use. Obedience is the foundation upon which our Christian faith rests. As I stated, Jesus said, "If you love me you will obey me."

Obedience is a conscious act of our wills. It is doing what we know God wants us to do. We must know God's word in order to obey it, and so obedience begins with the reading and study of the Bible. Scripture should become such a part of our being that when we are faced with a decision we just know what

Jesus would do because we know Him. I'm sure you know what your husband, children, or wife likes best: all their favorite food and TV shows, for example. Why? Because you spend time with them, you know them, and you want to please them. This is the same way we need to know God, and we will then find obedience much easier, though never easy.

Obedience
Reflection Questions and Advice

1. Is there a particular area of your life where you struggle with being obedient? What is it, and why do you believe it is such a struggle?

2. Ask God's forgiveness for this act of disobedience, and also ask Him for insight as to how you can take steps toward becoming more obedient. He wants to help us and He wants us to ask for His help.

3. Write in a journal about this area of struggle, and share it with a close and trusted friend. Ask this person to hold you accountable in your struggle; however, you must be willing to accept this person's role in this journey knowing you may not like his or her interference into your life.

4. Commit to memory the scripture verses that deal with obedience. The first one should be John 14:15: "If you love me you will obey what I command."

5. Is your desire to be obedient born out of a love for Jesus, or out of the fear of possible consequences?

- 2 -

FORGIVENESS

"Be gentle and ready to forgive: never hold grudges. Remember the Lord forgave you, so you must forgive others."
Colossians 3:13

It seems to make sense to follow the chapter on obedience with one on the topic of forgiveness. Why? Because our lack of obedience leads to our constant need to be forgiven. Again, I went to the dictionary, mostly to find out if forgiveness is still an acceptable English word, since being obedient has been relegated to children and pets, if they are so inclined. I was glad to see that the word "forgive" and all of its variations are still in the dictionary. But, what I found even more interesting was that the word "forgive" is directly preceded by the word "forget" in the New Oxford American Dictionary. Doesn't God have a great sense of humor? The word "forget" means "fail to remember," and "forgive" means "to stop feeling angry or resentful toward someone for an offense, flaw or mistake." I think that, as Christians, we often combine those two definitions to describe our own personal version of forgiveness: to fail to remember to stop feeling angry or resentful toward someone. Just a thought!

What Is Forgiveness?

Forgiveness was defined as "the action or process of forgiving or being forgiven." Now, that is more like it. A process or steps taken to achieve a specific end. No snap-of-the-fingers transformation. We need to remember that to forgive someone does not mean we are to excuse or ignore the hurt; it means we forgive because we have first been forgiven by Jesus. Our inexcusable behavior has been forgiven by God, so if we are to have the stamp of Christ on our lives, that would include forgiving the inexcusable behavior of others toward us.

Why Forgiveness?

There is a passage in the book of Matthew, from the Sermon on the Mount, where Jesus deals very clearly and directly with the issue of forgiveness. After teaching His disciples to pray, he says:

"For if you forgive men when they sin against you, your Heavenly Father will also forgive you. But if you do not forgive men their sins, your Father will not forgive your sins." (Matthew 6:14–15)

I don't know about you, but that verse has always been the one I come back to when my ability to forgive someone is totally unavailable to me, usually because I have absolutely no desire whatsoever to forgive. I would much rather wallow, plot revenge, and be generally very unloving and unlike Christ in my behavior. And then I remember how much I need to be forgiven, how much I have been forgiven, and I can begin the process of forgiving. The actress Carrie Fisher once said that resentment, which is the result of an unforgiving heart, is like drinking poison waiting for the other person to die. I believe that if we all stopped for one moment and gave some serious and concentrated thought to what Jesus really did for us on the cross, the idea of revenge or having an unforgiving heart would never even occur to us. But, we don't and it does.

As I did research for this book and the various topics I am covering, I, of course, googled each one. Now, for those of you who are not computer literate, to "google" means that you type the word "forgiveness" in the computer and every website in the universe and beyond, with the word "forgive/forgiven/forgiveness" in it, will become accessible to you. The quotation below is from one of the 1,660,000 websites that had a variation of the word "forgiveness" in their title. "We at the International Forgiveness Institute are dedicated to helping people gain knowledge about forgiveness and to use that knowledge for personal, group, and societal renewal." First of all, the fact that there is an international institute dedicated to forgiveness I found personally astounding. Nowhere on the website, however, was the name God, Jesus, Mohammed, Buddha, or any other person of spiritual significance mentioned. It did, however, reference all of the above as well as other sources for their four-step, scientific approach to forgiveness. The website made no mention of seeking forgiveness because of anything we may have done to offend God or anyone in our lives. Christians call this "sin," when they are inclined to acknowledge its existence. Their four step approach referenced only the need to forgive others for "a wrong done" Again, this appears to be the prevailing thought on the idea of forgiveness in our world today. If there is no absolute truth, then everything is acceptable and there is no "sin," so there is no need to seek or extend forgiveness. And if there is some absolute truth, I can't be held accountable for what I have done because of some parental abuse, genetic predisposition and a litany of other issues that remove all responsibility from me. We live in a society of victims. Oh, where it that simple!

There are, unfortunately, many preachers today who preach about God's love and having a positive attitude to the near exclusion of our responsibility as Christians. These are both important, but knowing God's word and what He expects from us as His followers is critical. Too many preachers and Christians don't talk about sin in its many forms because we don't want to upset or offend people. I believe hell is going to be very crowded with people we didn't want to offend. We all need forgiveness, and we are all sinners, all day and everyday. Now, let's admit it and begin to do something about it.

I have often said that two of the things we all have in common are death and sin. I don't know about your church, but most of the ones I have attended do not have these topics on their top-ten list of sermons. Why? They are unpleasant and someone will definitely be offended, especially when the pastor suggests that she has a sin issue in her life. It is that sin issue—and the blood Jesus shed as a price for our sin—that we need to be reminded of a lot more frequently that we are. I am not suggesting you put a sign on your mirror that says "Good morning, sinner," but I am suggesting we need to be reminded of why Jesus hung on the cross. A Protestant friend of mine has a crucifix in her home just for that purpose. Of course, the resurrection is important as well, but Jesus died to take our sin upon himself, and He rose to conquer that sin and give us eternal life.

When I first came to terms with my alcoholism and other addictions, I began attending an Alcoholics Anonymous (AA) meeting at my church. I had been told by someone that due to the depth of my problem, I would have to attend AA every day for the rest of my life. Now, that was sobering. I went for several months, although not every day, and came to see these meetings as an example of what church should be. I believe one of the many reasons AA works is because you are sitting in a room with people you know are in as bad a shape as you are, and many worse. Before you can speak in AA you must raise your hand, say your name, and then announce, "I am an alcoholic." The groups welcome you, and you then talk while they listen. I believe church should be called Sinners Anonymous, and, there we should have to raise our hands, and say our names followed by "I am a sinner."

Can you imagine how quiet our churches would become?

How to Forgive

When I first accepted Jesus as my Lord and Savior, I was biblically illiterate. I grew up in a household with an Irish Catholic father and a mother who said she was Jewish, and thought that God's last name was "damn it." So, when I read Mathew 18 and found out there was a limit on forgiveness, I was both delighted and terrified. I was delighted that my need to forgive stopped at seven times seventy (490 times), but terrified that my own forgiveness ended there as well. Upon further study, the seven times seventy is Jesus's way of saying forgiveness is unlimited, both in our giving it as well as receiving it. If that were not the case, I would have run out of this wonderful gift of God's in the spring of 1968.

Jesus's view of our willingness to forgive others or ask for it ourselves is best summed up at Matthew 18:35. Jesus discusses the man who was forgiven his debt because he begged his master to do so. Then, this man turned around, and one of his servants begged for him to forgive his debt. However, he would not forgive the debt, and he threw the man in jail. When this man's master heard what he had done, he immediately threw the man in jail because of his behavior. Matthew 18:35 says, "This is how my Heavenly Father will treat each of you unless you forgive your brother from your heart."

It is not enough that we forgive those who sin against us. It is not enough to ask God to forgive us when we sin against Him. What is enough is that both the act of extending forgiveness and asking for forgiveness must come from our heart. We must be honestly repentant and truly sorry for the hurt we have caused God and others. We must not ask for forgiveness just because scripture tells us to do so. While that is obviously a good place to start, we have to know and feel in our hearts that we need to be forgiven and to forgive. Forgiveness is a gift, freely given by God to all who come to Him and ask. We should be as willing to give the gift of forgiveness as freely as it has been given to us. When we know the joy and peace that comes with having been forgiven, whether by God or a person, we should not hesitate in offering the same gift that has been given to us.

The definition of forgiveness says we are to stop feeling angry. The editors of the New Oxford American Dictionary do not live in my house or even my world. I have always believed that feelings are fundamentally neutral. I have always believed that no one has the right to tell you how you should feel. They don't have to like how you feel, but I believe we need to respect one another's right to feel anyway we want. Of course, when we act on our feelings we can potentially affect others, and then, we need to be held accountable. If I feel like killing someone and act on that feeling, then I am responsible. But, it is much easier said than done when we read we are to stop feeling angry.

Who to Forgive

For some holding onto their anger and an unforgiving heart gives them a reason for getting out of bed every day. We all have heard someone say, "I will never forgive them." Those words scare me. As Jesus said, if we want to be forgiven I must first forgive. Holding a grudge is like holding a hot coal in your hand. The longer you hold it, the greater the damage. As Gandhi said, "The weak can never forgive. Forgiveness is the attribute of the strong." Asking for forgiveness does take courage, humility, and an acknowledgment that we have done something that requires forgiveness. It seems to be an act that benefits the one doing the forgiving more than the one being forgiven.

There are countless benefits in the act of forgiving someone. And to be sure forgiveness knows no religion but is an important and universal benefit to all mankind. Rabbi Eli Mallon listed in an article written for the Mayo Clinic Newsletter seven benefits from the act of forgiving someone.

Letting go of grudges and bitterness can make way for compassion, kindness and peace. Forgiveness can lead to:
* Healthier relationships
* Greater spiritual and psychological well-being
* Less anxiety, stress and hostility
* Lower blood pressure
* Fewer symptoms of depression and
* Lower risk of alcohol and substance abuse.
* Stronger immune system

- Improved heart health
- Higher self esteem

Now if these are the only reasons you are ever given to forgive someone, I believe they are more than enough.

Onetime, a friend of mine said that I needed to ask God to bring to mind people that I needed to forgive. I thought it a rather odd statement since I knew full well the people I had an unforgiving attitude toward. As we sat silently before God a most amazing thing happened. The Lord brought to my mind people that I had never even met. My father's parents were first. My grandmother died when my father was four years old and his father when he was sixteen, and, apparently, I harbored anger toward them for leaving my father. I especially felt this for his mother. Not that anyone chooses to die and leave a small child motherless, but something in me was angry with them and very sad for my father. You may be surprised at the people God will bring to mind.

I live in a suburb of Philadelphia, less than fifty miles from the town of Nickle Mines, PA, where in October 2006, a man entered an Amish schoolhouse and systematically shot and killed five young Amish girls. For those who are not familiar with the Amish people, they are a sect of Anabaptists who live their lives without any of the modern conveniences upon which we have come to depend. They have no electricity and drive no cars. They have horses and buggies and their local Wal-Mart has fifty buggy slots in its parking lot. The Amish, descendants of Swiss German settlers, are a Christian denomination and they place great importance on the gospel message of forgiveness. They believe in nonviolence, simple living, and little contact with the modern world. As the world of conveniences and technology crashes in on us, their lifestyle has enormous appeal. But, as the world watched in October of 2006, these very simple people in Nickel Mines, PA showed the world what Jesus was talking about when he said we should forgive others as we have been forgiven by Him.

These people demonstrated the true power of faith and forgiveness. "A pastor who had been with the family of the man who killed the children—the gunman left behind a wife and three children—told a Lancaster newspaper of being in the family's home when there was a knock on the door. It was an Amish neighbor coming on behalf of the community. He put his arms around Roberts's (the gunman) father and said, 'We will forgive you.' The pastor concluded: 'God met us in that kitchen'" (John Mark Ministries, www.jmm.org.au). A friend said to me at this time that the Amish were showing the world how Christians should live. They freely forgave someone that most of us would not be able to even consider forgiving. And, they did it with their hearts right before God while the rest of the world watched in disbelief and quiet envy at their Christ-like response. For this, we do not a four-step, scientific approach; as used by the International Forgiveness Institute. We only need Jesus.

The Blessings of Forgiveness

Forgiveness is an act of our will, and should be the desire of our heart. There have been studies done that show letting go of the anger and resentment that so often accompanies an unforgiving heart can lower your blood pressure, reduce stress, and generally improve your outlook on life. In a book by Everett Worthington, Jr., Five Steps to Forgiveness: The Art and Science of Forgiving, the author found that people who won't forgive the wrongs committed against them tend to have negative indicators of health and well-being, more stress-related disorders, lower immune-system function, and worse rates of cardiovascular disease than the population as a whole. In effect, by failing to forgive they punish themselves. Unforgiving people are also thought to experience higher rates of divorce, which also reduces well-being, given that married men and women consistently do better on most health barometers, including longevity.

Now, there is nothing fundamentally wrong with researching forgiveness, sin, or fly larvae. But, I believe that we too often look at research as a way of presenting us with reasons for doing or not doing something. We listen to movie critics, stock market analysts, read consumer reports, and restaurant critics, all in an effort to make sure we do the right thing, eat the right food, see the right movie. I do not believe that forgiving someone or asking for forgiveness has to be analyzed or explained.

We do it because Jesus tells us to do it. If there are

ancillary benefits to it, great! The Amish forgave the family of the man who killed five of their children. Why? They did it because they believe in the power and healing qualities of forgiveness. Because they believe that if Jesus tells them to do it that should be reason enough. As Oswald Chambers said, "Beware of reasoning about God's word—obey it." (Disciples Indeed, page 37) As Christians wanting to live our lives with the stamp of Christ on it, the fact that Jesus said it should be reason enough to do it. Many of us as parents have said to our children, who have questioned our reason for doing something, "Because I said so and I am the parent." Well, should our perfect Heavenly Father and Creator expect any less of us, His children?

The act of forgiving and being forgiven frees the soul and lightens our load. To wake up each and every morning knowing that a sacrifice has been made for every mean and sinful thing you will do for the next twenty four hours helps you to see the day more clearly

How Does This Work in My Everyday Life?

Just a few days ago, I had someone tell me, through tears and pain, "I will never forgive him!" She had a legitimate reason for saying this, but I tried to assure her not forgiving would only hurt her—not him. "Well, how can I do it?" That's the big question: how do I forgive? I believe we need to first acknowledge that in many cases we don't really want to forgive. We like being the martyr, and we like holding a grudge.

Somehow, if we forgive, we think what happens is that all the pain and what caused it ceases to exist. It does not. Forgiving others reduces our need and desire to seek revenge, and begins the process of being freed from the pain and hurt.

Just like obedience, forgiving is a conscious act of our wills and should not be judged by our emotions. I know I have been forgiven much, but I have not always felt forgiven. But, God says He does, so I accept that.

So, when you are faced with what seems like an insurmountable hurt, remember that our perfect, sinless Father forgives us all the time. Then, we need to extend that same forgiveness, grace, and mercy that He freely gives to us to those who have hurt us.

Forgiveness
Reflection Questions and Advice

1. Quietly, before God, ask to have those people you need to forgive brought to mind. Make a list of these people, and let go of the hurt and forgive them.

2. If there are people you need to ask forgiveness from, do so and record the date here. When you feel that anger creep up on you again, you can look and see the date you acted out of forgiveness.

3. Go out of your way to do something special for someone you have wronged.

4. Commit to memory scripture verses that have to do with forgiveness. Begin with Matthew 6:14–15.

- 3 -

CONFESSION

*"Therefore confess your sins to each other and pray for each other that
you may be healed."*
James 5:16

There are many who believe our society has lost its
moral compass and that there are fewer and fewer
things about which people feel any degree of shame or
embarrassment. As a result, there are fewer and fewer
reasons people feel the need to ask forgiveness. There
was a time in our society when being sixteen,
unmarried, and pregnant was not going to get you on
the cover of a national magazine. That has changed. I
agree that having the baby, regardless of the
circumstances, is better than abortion, but is having a
baby at sixteen years of age while unmarried
something we should celebrate? Apparently, it is.
There is no embarrassment, no shame, and, therefore,
no sin and no need for confession. There is a verse in
the Bible (Jeremiah 8:12) that speaks of a people that
"have no shame at all; they do not even know how to
blush…" My point is that things today are not that

much different that they were in biblical times; it is just that we see it and read about it while it is happening.

This may seem like eons ago, but in 1949, (after I was born), Ingrid Bergmann, the actress, and Italian director Roberto Rosellini, had an affair and she became pregnant. She was married to someone else, but left her husband. The public was outraged. The US Congress labeled Ingrid "an assault upon the institution of marriage" and "a powerful influence for evil." Our Congress today is made up of many people who believe men marrying men and women marrying women is just fine. A president having oral sex with a White House intern isn't fine, but not bad enough to punish him. It's just fodder for late night comedians. Can you believe Congress would even involve themselves in something like this? We should thank God they don't care today, or nothing would get done at all because they would be too busy labeling many of their own colleagues. But even though this was sixty years ago, the fact is that in just one generation we have gone from "a powerful influence for evil" to moral indifference. Sad, but true!

What Is Confession?

Confession, according to the New Oxford American Dictionary is, "1. a formal statement admitting one is guilty of a crime: 2. an admission or acknowledgement that one has done something that one is ashamed or embarrassed about." Based on this definition, if you haven't committed a crime or are not ashamed or embarrassed about anything you have done, there is no need for confession.

As usual, I googled the word "confession" and discovered there are several types. We have Protestant and Catholic confession of sins, confession of faith, and many more variations. I would have thought that references to Catholic confession would outnumber the Protestant ones, but they didn't. Catholic references reached 315,000, while Protestants registered 866,000. However, the term "confession of sins" garnered 4,620,000 hits. The winner and still champion! My personal favorite is the website www.confessions.grouphugs.us. You go to the website, and can write whatever you feel you need to confess. If you can't think of any, they have a list of potential infractions which may jog your memory. Once you confess, you click a button, get a hug, and everything is better. Oh, how I wish I were making this up, but I am not.

In a spiritual context, confession is generally thought of as a Catholic practice, one that is required before one may take Communion, and one that requires a priest as an intermediary between the sinner and God. An interesting aspect of this is the fact that the confessant says how long it has been since his last confession before he begins his litany of most recent confessable sins. The penance he will pay should somehow match the severity of the sins. Whether you agree with this practice or not it is a biblical mandate in James 5:16, and with it comes a promise. Not the confession to a priest part but the practice of confession as a part of your spiritual life. "Therefore, confess your sins to each other and pray for each other so that you may be healed."

I do not believe that James is speaking about indiscriminate confession, telling everybody everything, but we need to have someone in our life with whom we feel comfortable enough to share our deepest needs and sins without the fear of judgment or rejection. We need to have someone who can pray with us and for us. Someone who will hold our hurts and struggles close, and cover them with prayer. Most importantly, we need to come before our God with a repentant heart, confess our sins, and ask God's forgiveness. We also need to be willing to ask forgiveness of those against whom we have sinned.

Sin causes severe disturbances in our personal relationship with the Lord. Scripture says that the Holy Spirit is personally "grieved" and God's work "quenched" by our sin. As long as there is a rift in our relationship with God because of unconfessed sin, our spiritual growth and effectiveness as witnesses for Christ will be diminished. Once we confess, that breach is healed.

How Does Confession Look?

The word "confession" in the New Testament comes from the Greek word homologeo, meaning "to cite," "to name," or "to agree with." Confession is required by God to remind us of His authority in the matter of our lives. There are three steps to confession that we as Christians must be aware of.

First, we confess the sin. "But, if we freely admit that we have sinned, we find God utterly reliable and straightforward—He forgives our sins and makes us thoroughly clean from all that is evil" (I John 1:9). Secondly, we forget the sin. My brothers, I do not consider myself to have fully grasped it now. But, I do concentrate on this. I leave the past behind and with hands outstretched to whatever lies ahead I go straight for the goal—my reward the honor of my high calling by God in Christ Jesus" (Philippians 3:13–14). And, thirdly, isolate the sin. "See to it that no one misses the grace of God, and that no bitter root grows up to cause trouble and defile many" (Hebrews 12:15).

As Christians, I believe we have a tendency to determine our need for confession based on the seriousness of the sin. We call some lies little white lies meaning they are not too bad. I have never heard the phrase, big black lies, however. Others should be pretty obvious, but, unfortunately, we just don't seem to think we need to be willing to admit to a wrong. Therefore, there is no need to confess. I also think that our lack of honest confession is due to the fact that we are not attuned to the commandments Jesus lays forth in the New Testament. We do not know or again have forgotten all that is expected of us as Christians. Somehow, we think that if we keep the majority of the Ten Commandments, we will be okay. Not true. We are to be obedient to all ten, and the litany of commandments found in the New Testament as well as the rest of the Old Testament.

According to our society, abortion is legal; consequently, there should be no need to feel guilty. Adultery, while not encouraged, is certainly not something most people will confront others about. There are many things we do, often thoughtlessly, that under examination, we would see are wrong, hurtful, and separate us from God. These are the incidents in our lives that we need to confess. Any time we step outside of what we know to be God's will for our lives, as well as knowingly or unknowingly sin, our relationship with God is fractured. Like a broken bone, it can heal, but we must acknowledge the break, confess the sin, and ask for forgiveness.

How Does Confession Feel?

I think many of us have had the experience of confessing our sin to God, and suddenly feeling the weight of the world lifted from our shoulders. Now, why is that? As humans, we tend to allow things in our minds to take on a life of their own, and, in turn, they become much more important and larger in scope than they actually are. This does not mean some sins are worse than others, but it means that we treat them as though they are .We believe that if anyone, including God, hears about what we did, the earth will cease rotating and we will be the reason. So, when we finally get up the courage to admit what we have done, and confess it to God, and the world does not cease to rotate, we are relieved and feel as though the burden has been lifted.

Confession is not necessarily an emotional experience,

not accompanied by an emotional reaction. Your confession and God's forgiveness is based on His promise to cleanse you, and not on how you feel. Confession does not always remove our pain or suffering, but we must choose to live as though we know and believe we have been forgiven even when we don't feel so.

Why Do We Need to Confess?

How do we, as Christians, deal with our need to confess our sins? Do we deal with that need? Again, Jesus tells us to do it, and gives us a very specific reason and benefit to do so: "that you may be healed." It is understandable that we may not want to confess our sins to a friend, pastor, or even a total stranger, but we must understand that confession, repentance, and restoration are three very critical ingredients to a healthy spiritual life.

Below is the definition of confession found on Wikipedia, the online encyclopedia:

In the Christian faith the practice of confession is similar to the criminal one—to admit one's guilt. Confession of one's sins, or at least of one's sinfulness, is seen by most churches as a pre-requisite for becoming a Christian.

I read this to say that if we are Christians who practice confession, we are like criminals. However, if we look hard enough we might find a church where we can be Christians without needing to admit to being sinners.

You have to love this age of computer-generated religion.

One of my favorite characters in the Bible is David. Why? He was a scoundrel, sinner, adulterer, and murderer. And, he was all this while being a man after God's own heart and the apple of his eye. If you read Psalm 51, you will see what true confession is, and how David threw himself under the bus. He repented of his sin and begged for forgiveness all the time knowing he was not worthy. He begged God to cleanse him and create in him a pure heart. Now, when was the last time any of us fell prostrate before God and begged forgiveness? God asks us to be truly sorry because of our sin, but too often we aren't sensitive enough to even know we have sinned, or possibly we don't care enough to even ask God for forgiveness.

The Cost of Not Confessing Our Sins

A new Christian, or one who isn't daily in the word, may not know that it is possible to live out of fellowship with the Lord. It is also possible that he not know God's command that we confess our sin. In I John 1:6, John says, "If we claim to have fellowship with Him yet walk in darkness, we lie and do not live by the truth." Some people may not be spiritually sensitive enough to realize they are out of fellowship with the Lord. If you don't feel as close to the Lord as you once did or as close as you would like to be, ask yourself: who moved?

We all know Christians who continuously ignore the

commands we are given to confess our sin. We have all probably been that Christian at one time or another. God so desires that we have fellowship with Him and knows our sin prevents that, so He will use whatever He can to get us to the point of confession. Some of the more persuasive techniques He uses to encourage compliance are:

Loss of inner peace: (Phil. 4:6,7) "Do not be anxious about anything, but in everything, by prayer and petition, with thanksgiving, present your requests to God. And, the peace of God, which transcends all understanding, will guard your hearts and your minds in Christ Jesus."

Discipline: (Heb. 12:6) "Because the Lord disciplines those He loves and He punishes everyone He accepts as a son."

Conscience: (Heb. 13:18) "Pray for us. We are sure we have a clear conscience and desire to live honorably in every way."

Being sorry for our sin: (Psalm 32) "Blessed is he whose transgressions are forgiven, whose sins are covered."

So, these are some of the consequences of unconfessed sin. The most important benefit and blessing of our confession is that we have restored our fellowship with God.

Blessings of Confession

When we confess, the freedom we experience allows us to move forward rather than feel as though we are continuously weighed down with guilt. The Bible says, "He is faithful and just and will forgive us our sins and purify us from all unrighteousness. (I John 1:9) Confession requires that we have a sensitive spirit that lets us know that what we have done is wrong. It requires a conscience that is sensitive to what Jesus teaches, and not what our society says is right or wrong. I believe as our walk with the Lord matures and our knowledge of the word increases, the time between our sinning and asking forgiveness decreases in direct proportion. Our spirits and consciences become increasingly sensitive to the Lord, His will, and our desire to be obedient.

I heard a renowned psychologist say that he believed the majority of people in mental institutions could be restored to mental health if they knew and believed they were forgiven. There is no way to know if this is true, but confessing your sin, being forgiven, and forgiving others is a very powerful and freeing experience. One of the twelve steps in AA is to make amends for the pain we have caused others. This means confessing to what you have done and asking forgiveness from those we have wronged in any way. When I got sober, I figured I would spend the rest of my life on this step alone. But, what I discovered is that people are very eager to hear your confession and forgive. You have heard the expression that confession is good for the soul. Well, it is.

The more consistent we are in our confession of sin the closer and more intimate our walk with the Lord will be. Even though confession does not, by itself, cause a person to mature spiritually there can be no growth in the spirit if one has unaddressed sin and is out of fellowship with God. The ministry of the Holy Spirit requires unbroken fellowship, and Christian growth depends on the unhindered work of the Holy Spirit.

Confessing our sins and repenting opens the pathways to our Lord, whereas not confessing is like erecting a roadblock with no detour. One definition I heard of sin early in my Christian walk was any thought, word, or deed that separates us from God. As the Bible teaches, God sees us as sinless. Jesus sacrificed himself for us so that we could have communion with God. Sin for which there is no repentance and that is not confessed, for whatever reason, is saying that Jesus's sacrifice wasn't that big a deal. Let me assure you, it was a huge deal, and confessing our sin to God is just one way of saying we know that and are eternally grateful. The biblical scholar Matthew Henry once said, "Some people do not like to hear much of repentance; but I think it is so necessary that if I should die in the pulpit, I desire to die preaching repentance, and if I die out of the pulpit I would desire to die practicing it."

How Does This Work in My Everyday Life?

The first step in confession is the admission that we

have done something wrong. Then, we must ask God (or someone else) for forgiveness. It doesn't sound all that hard, but it is very, very hard. When my husband and I were married, the pastor said the seven most important words in a marriage are: "I'm sorry, I was wrong, please forgive me." And, we must remember when we need to say them, because doing it really does make for a healthier marriage.

But, confession is generally thought of as asking God directly for forgiveness, but in order to be able to do that we must know God's word. You won't know if you've sinned if you don't know what God expects of you. We know the big Ten Commandments, but what about feeding the hungry, taking in strangers, or giving a tenth of our riches to God? We tend to overlook these obligations, and leave them for others because "that's not my gift or calling." I'm not suggesting we must all do everything the Bible says, but we must be willing if God calls us to do it. By this I mean, some of the things God asks us to do may not be your particular gift, but it may be someone else's. I have learned that the better we know God's word and the closer we are to Him, the shorter the time between sinning and confession.

Confession
Reflection Questions and Advice

1. Find a still, quiet place and ask God to bring to mind those things in your life you need to confess. Write them down and seek forgiveness where appropriate.

2. Why do you think we are told to forgive?

3. What are some of the consequences for not forgiving?

4. Have you ever asked someone to forgive you and they wouldn't? What did you do?

5. Is there someone in your life you do not think you could ever forgive?

- 4 -

BE HOLY

"But just as He who called you is holy, so be holy in all you do; for it is written "Be holy because I am holy.""
I Peter 1:15

The word "holy" makes me very nervous and uncomfortable. I am not sure why, except that it isn't a word I have heard used a lot even in the most devout of Christian circles. We encounter it in scripture and songs used in reference to God, but I do not think I have ever heard it used in reference to a human other than Jesus. I am guessing there is a reason for that, and I think I know what that reason might be. And then I went to my trusty dictionary again and there it was. According to the New Oxford American Dictionary, holy means "dedicated or consecrated to God or a religious purpose; sacred; devoted to the service of God; morally or spiritually excellent."

So, having read that, it all falls into place why I have never heard this word used in reference to another human being. There are none of us worthy of the adjective, holy. None of us are morally or spiritually excellent. Consider this verse: "Don't let your character be molded by the desires of your ignorant days, but be holy in every department of your lives, for the one who has called you is himself holy. The Scripture says, 'Ye shall be holy for I am holy'" (I Peter 15–17).

What Is Holiness?

Holiness means to be set apart. To be holy is to be unique or uncommon. (Lev 10:10) Now, we all consider ourselves unique, but this uniqueness is the kind that causes eyebrows to rise and jaws to drop. God is holy. But, how do we as Christians live our lives in an everyday, holy way? In I Cor. 1:2, we are commanded to be holy. How is that possible and is the bar set too high? In scripture, holy is used in reference to God so we must look at God, imitate him, and we are beginning our journey to holiness. In Colossians 3:1–17, we have a practical guide for holy living. Practical doesn't mean easy.

As we read this verse, we see that we are being told to be holy because Jesus is holy, and if we want to live our life with the stamp of Christ on it, our lives must look like His. A Christian is a follower of Christ, one who lives his or her life according to the teachings of Jesus in the New Testament. So, is the only reason to be holy is because we are commanded to be? Or, should we want to be holy because we want to please our Heavenly Father and be like Him? We want to be a chip off the old block with the block being Jesus. We want to show our love for what He has done for us by being obedient, and obedience manifests itself by doing as He asks. "Be holy because I am holy."

It is also true that all who have put their faith in Jesus Christ are holy. But, this should be considered only the first step toward a life that is seen as holy. We should be holy because:

- Our life was designed by God to be set apart for Him.
- Sin, which seems pleasurable, leads to self-destructiveness, pain, and death.
- Living in a way that reflects who we are leads to joy and a fullness of life.
- We have been chosen by God himself to be an example of His love and grace.
- Desiring holiness is our way of showing God our grateful hearts for the gift of His son and our salvation.
- Knowing God better requires that we live our life on His terms, not our own.
- God commands us to be holy.

But, being obedient and wanting to be holy doesn't necessarily make it so. In 2 Corinthians 7:1, Paul says, "Since we have these promises, dear friends, let us purify ourselves from everything that contaminates body and spirit, perfecting holiness out of reverence for God." The promises he is referring to are those at the end of 2 Corinthians 6:17 and 6:18. He calls us to be separate, touch nothing unclean, and He will be our

Father.

How Do We Become Holy?

This is really a steep mountain to climb, which is why the first thing we need to do is to get on our knees and ask the God to take us by the hand, and lead us in the direction of the holiness He asks of us. In order to be holy we must first understand what holy is, and our example is Jesus Christ, our Savior, our Master, our everything. Holiness is a state that is not attainable here on earth, but one we are expected to, at the very least, move toward as we walk our Christian walk. Holiness means we are to have the same mind set as Christ, to know and follow His ways, His precepts, and His plan for our lives. Even with this mindset, we will still face struggles with our sinful nature, but these are the struggles that will produce a depth and holiness as we learn to respond to God within the realities of our life.

We are to put to death our earthly nature which includes sexual immorality, impurity, lust, evil desires, greed, anger, rage, malice, slander, filthy language, and lying. And, once we have done that we are to clothe ourselves with compassion, kindness, humility, gentleness, patience, forbearance, and forgiveness. We must then bind them all together in perfect unity with the virtue of love. Be thankful, letting the word of Christ dwell in your hearts. Sing songs and psalms of praise with gratitude in your heart, and do all of this in the name of the Lord.

In Ephesians 4:22, we are told to "put on the new self, created to be like God in true righteousness and holiness." Holiness seems to be a major byproduct of obedience, forgiveness, and confession. As the definition says, we are to be "morally or spiritually excellent." This is a journey that consists of one step forward, two steps back, but as long as we make small but deliberate steps forward, we will be able to stand before God knowing we have done the best we can, with His help.

As Paul says in Romans 6:19,
"I put this in human terms because you are weak in your natural selves. Just as you used to offer the parts of your body in slavery to impurity and to ever-increasing wickedness, so now offer them in slavery to righteousness leading to holiness."

Righteous means "acting in accord with divine or moral law; free from guilt or sin." We all agree with what is said here, but when we are called to live it out in our everyday world, then it becomes another issue. We know we cannot be guilt free or sin free, but we actually try to steer the boat in that direction. How often do we go along to get along? "How often do we know what the Lord would have us do in a particular situation, but still resist doing it?" We don't want to offend someone. Hell is going to be filled with people we did not want to offend. If we all had to have our spiritual houses in order before we could speak out, no one would ever say anything. I don't believe anyone can ever achieve any degree of holiness in a vacuum.

The Christian scholar, author, and leader, John Stott,

wrote in a book entitled Involvement: Being a Responsible Christian in a Non-Christian Society. He describes four truths of the Christian faith that cannot be missed.

1. Christians are fundamentally different from non-Christians.
2. Christians must permeate non-Christian society.
3. Christians can influence non-Christian society.
4. Christians must retain their Christian directness.

He uses the metaphor of salt and light to illustrate these truths. We don't need to be reminded of how dark the world can be at times. But, as Christians, are we providing the light that people are looking for? Are we allowing our saltiness to prevent further decay in society? God has called us out and set us apart to be a direct and powerful force for good in a fallen world. Being set apart is one of the definitions of holiness. Are you salty enough to make people thirst for the living water of Jesus Christ? Is your light bright enough to pierce the darkness? Jesus was called "the light" and, in John 9:5, He says, "I am the world's light as long as I am in it." As He no longer walks as He once did, we have become the children of light. In John 12:36, He says, "Put your trust in the light while you have it, so that you may become sons of light."

Some ask these questions: Is holiness a way of life or an attitude? Is holiness making sure we follow all the rules or being a special type of person? To be holy is to be a follower of Jesus Christ, one who lives his life in obedience to His teachings, and lives a life of faith, love, and hope. It is not enough to just be a doer of good deeds.

Some Christians feel that we are to separate ourselves from society in order to be set apart. Well, yes, we must be set apart in the way we live our lives, in our attitudes and desires, and in our behavior. But, we must also live as Christians in society if we have any chance of drawing people to the Lord we serve. Light serves no purpose if it is hidden under a basket, and salt does no good if it is kept in its container. We are to be salty enough to make others thirsty for the living water, and our light is to be bright enough for people to see the Lord. These are definite steps on the journey to the holiness Jesus calls us to. We must also realize that light will uncover and illuminate all the sins and flaws we try so hard to cover up.

What Does Holiness Look Like?

As Paul says in Philippians 2:5, "Your attitude should be the same as that of Christ Jesus." That seems pretty clear to me, but the day-to-day living out of that verse can be at the very least overwhelming. Jesus is everything I am not, but all that I strive to be. He is holy, trustworthy, pure, blameless, and the same always. He has been sacrificed and set apart by God, so that we can let God set us apart for His use in this world. Consider Hebrews 12:14: "Make every effort to live in peace with all men and to be holy; without holiness no one he will see the Lord." As Christians, we need to separate ourselves from what God hates, and attach ourselves to what He loves and what we need to do. (I Romans 12:1–2; 2 Cor. 7:1; Phil. 2:14–15)

Holiness should be our identity. Peter says, "Dear friends, I urge you, as aliens and strangers in the world, to abstain from sinful desires, which war against your soul. Live such good lives among the pagans that, though they accuse you of doing wrong, they may see your good deeds and glorify God on the day that He visits us" (I Peter 2: 11–12).

We are new creatures who belong to another kingdom, but we are creatures who should stick out in any crowd because of the way in which we live our lives. We should stick out because of who we are in a holistic way, not because of a few specific things we don't do, or things we do. The light and love of Christ should shine through every aspect of our lives, thought, word, and deed, and draw others to Him. That is holiness.

We cannot earn holiness. It is a gift from God. In Exodus, God speaks to Moses and tells him to observe the Sabbath. God tells him that, "This will be a sign between me and you for generations to come, so you may know that I am the Lord who makes you holy" (Ex 31:13). Holiness is taking the words of Jesus seriously. Being holy may look different depending on the situation; it could mean dressing modestly, forgiving an abuser, not cutting people off in traffic, or starting a home for unwed mothers. Whatever the hat we are called to wear, it should look like a halo to the rest of the world.

Blessings of Being Holy

I think most of us would agree with the principle that we, as Christians, should strive to be holy. I believe we would also agree that it will be a long, uphill climb that will not see its completion and perfection this side of heaven. Imagine being asked the question, "What is on your agenda for the day?" Most of us would not answer, "I am going to continue my journey to becoming holy." Even though we know in our hearts and heads that none of us will ever achieve the holiness God asks of us, we also know there is hope; God is gracious and will help us every step and misstep along the way.

In I Corinthians 6:11, Paul lists several unholy acts, and then says, "But, you were washed. You were sanctified, you were justified in the name of the Lord Jesus Christ and by the Spirit of our God." When we put our faith in Jesus, our only hope for forgiveness, He cleanses us and declares us His child, holy and set apart for His service. This holiness is not ours because we have earned it, but because we have placed our complete trust and reliance in Christ.

Perhaps the greatest blessings we receive from our attempts to be holy is the knowledge that we have pleased the God who sacrificed it all for us. It is knowing that we have brought joy to the heart of Him who loves us most. It is the joy we experience when we see and feel that our lives are actually moving in the right direction (for a change). We are blessed by granting God our complete, undivided, and unbridled love and obedience. As we become more and more like Him in the way we choose to live our lives, we bring Him joy and we in turn experience joy.

I spoke to a group of high school students at a leadership conference and used the following example. I showed them the owner's manual to my husband's Harley-Davidson motorcycle. I told them it was written by the people who made his bike, so if my husband wants his bike to run long and well, he will do what the manual says. So it is with the Bible. I picked up the Bible and said, "This is our owner's manual, written by our owner, who purchased us with His own blood."

If we, as Christians, want to run long and well, then we need to follow the manual. We need to take the words of Jesus seriously.

How Does This Work in My Everyday Life?

The Bible, at, I Peter 1:15 says, "Be ye holy because I am holy." That's the *why* of being holy. The following is an account of the how.

Like so many of these commandments, there are no simple answers as to how they translate into our everyday life. Holiness is a goal, a process, a long and difficult journey. It must be the desire of our heart to seek the holiness God asks of us, while all the time knowing our chances of fully attaining it this side of heaven are not very good. Take the hand of Jesus and move everyday in the direction of His love and grace.

Be Holy
Reflection Questions and Advice

1. Have you ever thought seriously about the concept of holiness? If so, what are your first thoughts when you hear the word?

2. What one change could you make to your life today to take a step closer to the holiness God asks of us?

3. How can we, as Christians, encourage one another to live a life that is holy?

4. What do you think your world would do if you took living a life of holiness seriously? By your world, I mean family, friends, and coworkers, et cetera.

5. Do you believe in your heart that we are not worthy of the gift of holiness?

- 5 -

PRAYER

"Be joyful always, pray continually; give thanks in all circumstances."
I Thessalonians 5:16

What Is Prayer?

Prayer is defined in the New Oxford American Dictionary as "a solemn request for help or expression of thanks addressed to God or an object of worship." I am going to assume that the majority of people reading this book will address their prayers to God. Prayer comes from the Latin meaning "obtained by entreaty" (an earnest or humble request). Prayer is an intimate form of communication between a child and his Father. Prayer is a conversation. Prayer is our way of getting to know God better, and as scripture says, we are to pray without ceasing. (I Thess. 5:17)

As Christians, we seem to view prayer as a normal, everyday event in our lives, in which we have fleeting or in-depth conversations with God. We may be looking for a parking space in the mall, or seeking healing for a dying child. The content of our prayers may vary, but our desire remains pretty much the same—we need help and we are asking our Heavenly Father for that help. We pray for help, we give thanks in our prayers, we pray for forgiveness, and we sometimes just pray, knowing that God is always there and always listening. Sometimes, we just need someone to talk to, so why not talk to someone who can actually do something?

Why Do We Pray?

We are commanded in James 5:13–18 to pray. We are told to pray if we are in trouble, pray our thanks for the good we have been given, pray for the sick, admitting your sins in prayer, pray for the power that is made available when we pray. Corrie Ten Boom, , a Dutch Christian who saved Jews from the Holocaust, asks, "Is prayer your steering wheel or your spare tire?" For many of us, prayer is not always the first thing we think to do when good or bad things happen to us. The first thought is usually, "How can I fix this?" For many of us, prayer is an afterthought when it should be a first thought. Paul wrote the following, at I Thessalonians 5:17–18, to the church at Thessalonica:

"Be happy in your faith at all times. Never stop praying. Be thankful, whatever the circumstances may be. If you follow this advice you will be working out the will of God expressed to you in Christ Jesus."

Well, that is easy for Paul since he wasn't living with a

spouse, or dealing with a boss, and he wasn't struggling with unemployment and the mother of all recessions. No, but Paul was addressing people who were being persecuted for their faith by the Jews. We know how that ended for Jesus, so let's imagine that what these early Christians were experiencing was as bad or worse than what any of us have gone through or ever will go through.

These verses don't just tell us to pray regardless of what is happening in our life, but they tell us what happens if we heed the advice. We will be working out the will of God expressed to us in Christ Jesus. Isn't that what this Christian journey is all about? We need not ask what is God's will for our lives, but what is God's will. The answer to that question is what we are to do, and knowing His will comes from reading His word and listening to Him as we pray.

We should want to pray if for no other reason than it is time communicating intimately with the person who knows us best and loves us most. We should want to pray because this same person wants what is best for us more than we want it for ourselves, and treasures the times we come to Him as His child, seeking His guidance. How do we feel as parents when our children of any age ask us for advice? How do we feel as they grow and mature and come to us less and less for advice or anything else? As much as we love our children, we can't comprehend the degree to which our Heavenly Father loves us.

In Philippians 4:6–7, Paul commands, "Be anxious

about nothing, but in everything, by prayer and petition, with thanksgiving, presents your requests to God. And, the peace of God, which transcends your understanding, will guard your hearts and minds in Christ Jesus." Prayer is the best anti-anxiety medicine there is. Knowing that you have come before the Father with your requests, prayers, and praises will allow you to relax and know that God has heard your prayers, and will answer them in the way that is best for you.

A. W. Tozer said, "Prayer will become effective when we stop using it as a substitute for obedience." Once again, the issue of obedience becomes the platform for the strength of our Christian walk.

How Do We Pray?

I have always thought of prayer as a conversation with my Creator. I have also come to understand that nothing I can say to God will come as a surprise to Him.

Gandhi said, "Prayer is not an old woman's idle amusement. Properly understood and applied, it is the most potent instrument of action." Prayer changes things. Too often we will thoughtlessly say to someone, "I'll pray for you." But, do we say it because we mean it and will do it, or because we think this is what we are supposed to say? In his book, Reaching for the Invisible God, Philip Yancey says to become a master in prayer requires only an intense desire to spend time with God. (page 39)

Scripture does teach us how to pray. In Matthew 6 Jesus is asked by His disciples to teach them how to pray. He tells them to not pray like play-actors who love to stand and pray in the synagogues and on street corners. We should go into our prayer closets, shut the door, and pray quietly to our Father. He then teaches them the Lord's Prayer. I do not believe that we need be as concerned with the form of our prayers as we are the content. Matthew 6 also says that our Heavenly Father knows our needs before we ask Him. This may raise the question: why do we need to pray at all if God already knows our needs. Because God tells us to, and this is the way we get to know Him better. When we pray if we have faith the size of a mustard seed whatever we ask God will do.

When my youngest son was a baby he had been very sick with a high fever and cough. I took his temperature over three days and it was hovering around 103 degrees. I called the doctor who said if it didn't drop before bedtime, we would have to bring him to the hospital. As he slept in my arms, I sat at the dinner table and asked his brother, who was nearly three years old, to pray for his brother. Without losing a beat, David prayed, "Dear Jesus, please thank God for making Peter better. Amen!"

Well, the mustard-seed-sized prayer of the child was answered immediately. Peter lifted his head, the redness drained out of his face, and he ate for the first time in three days. As the adults at the table cried, David asked what was wrong. I said, "Did you see

71

Peter? He is better." He replied, "Isn't that what you wanted?" The prayers of a child. The faith of a child. It never occurred to him that God would not answer his prayer. The thing I will never forget about that prayer was how David asked Jesus to thank God for answering his prayer. It was a simple thank you for doing what he was asking. So often, we get hung up on the words of our prayers, wanting to sound just right. In Matthew 6:5–8, Jesus speaks very specifically about how we are to pray.

But, when you pray, do not be like the hypocrites, for they love to pray standing in the synagogues and on the street corners to be seen by men. I tell you the truth, they have received their reward in full. When you pray, go into your room, close the door, and pray to your Father, who is unseen. Then, your Father, who sees what is done in secret, will reward you. And, when you pray, do not keep babbling like pagans, for they think they will be heard because of their many words. Do not be like them, for your Father knows what you need before you ask Him.

One of the best books I have read on the subject of prayer is by Prayer: Key to Revival, by Paul Y. Cho. I used this book for my quiet time many years ago, and through the book, my time with the Lord, and scripture I learned a lot about prayer. Jesus teaches us how to pray by the example he sets in His own prayer life. In Matthew 14;23, Jesus "went up on a mountainside by Himself to pray. In Luke 11:1, "Jesus was praying in a certain place." And, near the end of His life, Jesus said, "Sit here while I go over there and pray" (Matt 26:36). Jesus tells us to pray regularly without ceasing.

One morning, during my quiet time, I was reading this book, and Paul Cho said to pray with specificity. If you want a red car pray for a red car. Well, this particular morning I wanted my dog that had been missing for three days to come home. I had looked everywhere, called vets, the SPCA, and done everything I knew to do to find my dog. So, I decided to pray boldly and specifically. "Dear God, please have Rusty on our deck by six a.m. Thank you." And, I continued on with my quiet time. Well, you know full well what happened—at 6:00 a.m. there was my dog, who had not been seen for three days, wagging his tail as if to say, "Someone said you were looking for me." Prayer works. The most common cause of unanswered prayer is prayerlessness. As is written in James 4:2, "You do not have, because you do not ask." We must learn, as Christians, that we need to learn to pray with expectations, great purpose, and with passion. God wants to hear from us, regardless of the circumstances.

I had a serious back injury as a child, which followed me the rest of my life. For those of you with chronic back pain, you know what I mean when I say that when your back hurts, everything hurts. Now, there was only so much I could do: pills, braces, exercises, et cetera. One day while chatting with a friend, she asked me if I ever asked God to heal me. What a concept! No, that avenue had yet to be traveled, not because I didn't think God could or would heal me, but I just never did it. Duh! Well, on my knees I said, "God, I would like you to take away now and forever all the back pain I have suffered. Thank you. Amen." It was as if He was just waiting for me to ask so He could say, "of course I will." And, He did. That was twenty years ago, and unless I work outside in the yard thinking I can do the things I did at twenty-five, I am fine, all day, and every day. Prayer works, and our Heavenly Father wants us to come to Him with all our requests.

Blessings of Prayer

There are several ways we, as Christians, get to know God better, and one of those is our time in prayer. Prayer is one of the ways we communicate with God, and He with us. Someone said once that talking to God is prayer, and God talking to us means we are crazy. Not true! Two-way communication is one means for two people to get to know each other. God gave us one mouth and two ears, so I am guessing He wants us to listen twice as much as we speak. True, God already knows us better than we know ourselves, but He wants us to come to Him asking, thanking, and praising. Just as we love it when our children come to us for advice, help, or just to share, so too Jesus loves when His children ask for His help. Prayer is an important way we get to know, God and He gets to know us. Of course, he knows us already, just as we know our children, but doesn't it make us feel good, needed, and loved when our children come to us to talk?

In his book, Prayer: Does it make a Difference?, Philip

Yancey says that during the research for his book he continually found a gap between prayer in theory and prayer in practice. If you ask your Christian friends how important is prayer in their life, I am guessing most would say very important. Then, ask them how much uninterrupted time they spend on their knees each day, and I think you will find a huge gap in theory and practice. Now, you don't have to get calloused knees. You can pray anytime, anywhere, but if Jesus is the example for us to follow, most of us fall woefully short of that example. Jesus knew that without God he could do nothing. We must know this and act accordingly. There are numerous places in scripture where Jesus separates himself from the disciples and his followers to go off and pray. (For example, read Matthew 14.23; Matthew 26:36; Mark 6:46; and Mark 14:32) Again, this is the example we are to follow. There is no gap in theory and practice with Jesus. And, there should be no gap, or an ever-decreasing gap, between our own theory and practice.

Philip Yancey also says in his book something I hadn't thought about, but now realize is true and transforming.

If prayer stands as the place where God and human beings meet, then I must learn about prayer. Most of my struggles in the Christian life circle around the same two themes: why doesn't God act the way we want God to, and why don't I act the way God wants me to? Prayer is the precise point where those two themes converge.

Our desire to become more like Christ should be the paramount goal of our lives as Christians. We need to take the words of Jesus seriously.

In his book, Too Busy Not to Pray, Bill Hybels says:

"Authentic Christianity is not learning a set of doctrines, and then stepping in cadence with people all marching the same way. It is not simply humanitarian service to the less fortunate. It is a walk—a supernatural walk—with a living, dynamic, communicating God. Thus, the heart and soul of the Christian life is learning to hear God's voice, and developing the courage to do what he tell us to do."

In order to hear God's voice we must be still and listen. So often we aren't sure if the voice we hear is God, or our own desires. How do we know the difference? I think we know instinctively when those urges we experience are from our Heavenly Father, and when they are from our earthly, selfish egos. If we aren't sure, as with most things, we can test it against scripture. If it stands that test, then one can be fairly certain that the urge is from above. The blessing comes from knowing we are living out our life in the will of God.

In the early 1990s, there was the WWJD (What Would Jesus Do?) movement. I am not so sure it was a movement as much as a fad and a way to sell rubber wristbands, but eventually it became a catch phrase for Evangelical Christian youth. It was so overexposed that the saying became trite and almost meaningless. But, the intent was what we should all have as our guiding principle. In reaction to this WWJD, came FROG (Fully Rely on God). Also, not a bad piece of advice. Relying on God and doing what we know Jesus would do is its own reward in so many ways. "If you love me you will obey my commandments" (I John 5:3).

If you read through the New Testament and make a list of all the things Jesus either did, or told His followers to do, there is your road map. There is the blueprint for your life. Sounds easy, but it's not! I know we all know this, but Jesus was God. Yes, Jesus. He is the one who knows all, sees all, hears all, and loves and forgives all. We are not Him. We are the reason God sent Jesus. All through the Old Testament, God tried to communicate with man and He didn't have much luck. Floods, plagues, fire, locust—you name it and it happened. The people didn't get what He was trying to do. So, in order to communicate with us, God sent Jesus—someone who looked like us. Jesus was God, but with skin on. And, even his brother James didn't get the message right away. Somehow, I want to believe that if I grew up in the same house with Jesus I would notice a difference between Him and me. Sounds reasonable, right? Well, not for James.

In the book The Prayer that Changes Everything, author Stormie Omartian talks about the fact that worship and praise are the purest forms of prayer, because both allows us to focus on Jesus and not ourselves. Too often our prayers become all about us, while worship and praise are all about Him. If we were able to truly understand who God really is, our prayers, praise, and worship would not be able to be contained. We would be in awe, spellbound, blown away by the majesty and holiness of God.

The main blessing of prayer is getting to know, in an intimate and personal way, the Creator of the universe. That should be enough! And, if we really believed in our heart of hearts that we could get to know the Creator of the universe, we probably would take prayer more seriously. But, I don't think we do. Our finite minds cannot grasp fully the love and relationship we could have with our God and Savior.

There is an old hymn, "What a Friend we have in Jesus," written in 1855. I heard it the other day and realized that it answers the question regarding what the blessings of prayer are. Here it is.

What a friend we have in Jesus,
All our sins and griefs to bear!
What a privilege to carry
Everything to God in prayer!
Oh, what peace we often forfeit,
Oh, what needless pain we bear,
All because we do not carry
Everything to God in prayer!

Have we trials and temptations?
Is there trouble anywhere?
We should never be discouraged—
Take it to the Lord in prayer.
Can we find a friend so faithful,

Who will all our sorrows share?
Jesus knows our every weakness;
Take it to the Lord in prayer.

Are we weak and heavy laden?
Cumbered with a load of care?
Precious Savior, still our refuge—
Take it to the Lord in prayer.
Do thy friends despise, forsake thee?
Take it to the Lord in prayer!
In His arms He'll take and shield thee,
Thou wilt find a solace there.

Blessed Savior, Thou hast promised
Thou wilt all our burdens bear;
May we ever, Lord, be bringing
All to Thee in earnest prayer.
Soon in glory bright, unclouded,
There will be no need for prayer.
Rapture, praise and endless worship
Will be our sweet portion there.

How Does This Work in My Everyday Life?

You've heard that if we talk to God we are praying, but if God is talking to us we are crazy. Well, I am delighted that I can talk to God, but even more delighted when He decides to talk to me. Do I hear a voice like James Earl Jones? Does the earth move, followed by flashes of light and clapping thunder? Nope! None of that. Praying is when we talk to God and share our heart with Him. As we said earlier, God is our Father and as a parent He wants us to come to

Him, just as we want our children to come to us.

Prayers are answered and God talks to us through scripture, friends, family, and sometimes even strangers. God talks to us in many ways; we just need to be listening. When He tells us to pray without ceasing He is saying let prayer be an attitude of your heart. Pray while walking, cooking, driving, and doing laundry. Whenever and wherever you are. God is there and He wants to hear from us.

Prayer
Reflection Questions and Advice

1. What do you most need to change about your prayer life?

2. Have you ever had a very specific answer to a prayer that could only have come from God?

3. What are the three answers to our prayers? How do you deal with them?

4. Is there a prayer you have been saying for what seems like forever that has yet to be answered? Why do you think this is the case?

5. What are some of the hindrances to unanswered prayer?

- 6 -

TRUST

"Do not be anxious about anything, but in everything, by prayer and petition, with thanksgiving, present your requests to God."
Phillipians 4:6

Trust is a word that by its mere mention causes emotions begin to run high. Do you trust me? Can I trust you? When you trust someone you can tell them anything, and you are not afraid to be open and vulnerable with that person. Trust is one the main and most important ingredients in a relationship. We all have people in our lives that we expect we can trust, but then something goes wrong and we find out we can't. Let's go back to the dictionary for the meaning of the word.

What Is Trust?

According to the New Oxford American Dictionary, trust means "to believe in the reliability, truth, ability or strength of. To allow someone to have, use, or look after someone or something of importance or value with confidence." In Jeremiah 17:5, the Lord says, "Cursed is the one who trusts in man, who depends on flesh for his strength and whose heart turns away from the Lord."

Most of us know that our friends and family are trustworthy, but only to a point. We all want to believe that our husbands and wives are totally and completely trustworthy, but the truth is we are all fallen and sinful human beings who have feet of clay. Without the help of the Lord, we all have the potential to break the trust we have established with those in our life. The only place our trust is safe is in the Lord. "It is better to trust in the Lord that to put confidence in man" (Psalm 118:8). Every word of God is pure: "He is a shield unto them that put their trust in Him" (Proverb 30:5). And, the list goes on of promises in scripture.

The dictionary definition seems rather pedestrian and simple. I trust my husband with our children, I trust my mother will not forget my birthday, and I trust my friends to care for me when I am sick. Whatever the situation, trust is a necessary and integral part of any relationship. If there is no trust, there is no relationship. In the King James version of the Bible there are 147 verses using the word "trust." Of these, 134 are in the Old Testament, and thirteen are in the New Testament. What is the significance of the disparity in the number of uses of the word "trust"? In the Old Testament, the people were commanded to trust a God they could not see and did not always feel was present in their lives. In the New Testament, Jesus is very present, very visible, and in some ways much easier to trust. The uses of the word "trust" are essentially the same, asking us to put our trust in God and Jesus. "Anyone who puts his trust in Him will never be put to shame" (Romans 10:11). So, here we have the commandment from Jesus, which has a promise attached. Trust in Him and you will never be put to shame. Using the definition above, we have put our souls, lives, hearts, and minds into the trusting hands of Jesus. We do it with the confidence that He is worthy of that trust. Or, have we? To trust another means we have faith in the fact that they will handle the relationship with the importance it needs. However, the trust among people can and often is broken with a misplaced word, a betrayal, or an unintentional hurt. Each time we have our trust in another broken, we are hesitant to trust as easily again. Trust can and often is rebuilt, but it takes time and sometimes it just can't be done.

I have heard people say, "I will trust someone until they give me reason not to." That is fine unless the person is inherently untrustworthy to start with. I started this book with a chapter on obedience because I feel that is the foundation upon which our faith stands. If we aren't going to be obedient to the Lord, does any of the rest matter? However, our obedience must be based on our belief that the Lord can be trusted in every way and completely. Why would we be obedient to someone we couldn't trust? We wouldn't.

There are many examples of people in the Bible who blindly and obediently put their trust in God. Abraham is one of the first. God asked Abraham to "leave your country, your people, and your father's household and go to a land that I will show you" (Genesis 12:1). Now, along with this order, God also told him that he would "make you a great nation, make your name great, you will be a blessing and all the people of the earth will be blessed through you" (Genesis 1:2–3). So, Abraham was willing to put his trust in God, but obviously he also believed he would be greatly blessed and rewarded for this trust. And, he was!

Another example was Ruth, daughter-in-law of Naomi. Much like Abraham, Ruth learned to not just love Naomi, but to love and trust her God. There is no indication that Ruth was a believer in God before she married Naomi's son. Once her husband died, Ruth was encouraged by Naomi to return to her family and what she knew. In a passage we all are familiar with, Ruth says to Naomi, "Where you go I will go, and where you stay I will stay, your people will be my people and your God, my God..." (Ruth 1:16–17). Ruth had come to believe and accept the God of Naomi, even after all the pain and suffering Naomi had endured.

These are just two examples, but from each act of trust and obedience came a history-changing event. Abraham did become the father of many nations, both Jew (Isaac) and Arab (Ishmael), and Ruth married Boaz who was the father of Obed, who was the father of Jesse, who was the father of David, who was in the line of Jesus Christ our Savior. One woman's love and trust in God allowed her to become the great grandmother to King David. Again, the trust Ruth and

Abraham had was rooted in their deep love of God, and a desire to be obedient to His teachings.

Well, this is all well and good, you say, but you are neither Ruth nor Abraham. You are Cathy from Kansas, and if you lived out this kind of trust and obedience in your world today, you would be quietly scoffed at for being naïve and too trusting. And, somewhere deep inside you, you might almost agree. But, in spite of the difficulty we have with complete surrender and obedience, we know through example and experience that what scripture teaches is true.

Have you ever thought about the fact that the stories, parables, and events we read about in the Bible were not there for those people in the Old Testament and for most of those people in the New Testament? And, what about Noah? Look what he did. He built a boat in the desert. Why? Because God told him to and he trusted God. We have what should be an advantage knowing how the story ends, but it doesn't seem to help that much. We still struggle and doubt, question God, fight with God, and do battle daily with our sinful nature. In 2 Samuel 22:31, the author (unknown) reminds us, "As for God, His way is perfect; thy Word of the Lord is tried: He is a buckler to all that trust in Him."

Why is it so hard for us to trust, not just God, but anyone? You have probably heard that little children have complete trust in the adults in their lives. This is what enables them to laugh with glee as they are thrown in the air by their parent and then caught.

What would happen if they were either intentionally or accidently dropped? Chances are there would be less laughter and glee the next time this happened. Trusting means we have to relinquish control of our lives, believing that those people to whom we have relinquished are trustworthy. Now, we know not all people are trustworthy all the time, but we do know that God is trustworthy all the time. You cannot find any place in scripture where God says, "oops" or where He doesn't do exactly what He says He will every time.

There is, not surprisingly, a website that is the king of the how-to instruction. One section is on how to build trust. Now, don't get me wrong, these websites can be helpful as long as we realize that they are just that— websites. But, there are nineteen steps it recommends you take to build trust. All of the steps are good and valid, but as Christians we could just follow the ninth commandment: "you shall not give false testimony against your neighbor" (Ex 20:16). In other words, be a person who can be trusted. I remember an older Christian saying to me long ago that if we followed the Ten Commandments, there would be no need for any other laws. I believe that.

How does being a person who relies totally on Jesus look in our twenty-first-century world? The issue of trust is cemented in the reality of our faith. You cannot separate them. You must trust God to have complete faith not only in His existence, but in the fact that He is always there and always right. Now, the next step in this journey is putting that trust and faith into action.

We live in a society and world where self-sufficiency is applauded and independence is the goal. We live in a society where there don't seem to be any moral absolutes, everything is all right, no one is to blame for anything, and as long as you don't really hurt anyone you just live your life. So, here we are, putting our faith in someone or something that can't be seen, smelled, touched, or heard. We are a fish out of water and swimming upstream, against the tide of anything society thinks is even remotely normal. But, we look through the Bible and we see example after example of times when people put their total trust and faith in the Lord, acted in obedience when it didn't seem logical, and God was faithful. He is faithful. He is real. He is there. And, He is right all the time.

The best way to live out your faith and trust in the Lord is to take steps toward Him every day. Walk to God to walk with Him. He wants nothing more from us than our love, faith, and trust, which leads to obedience, which leads to the life He has planned for us. "I know what I am doing. I have it all planned out—plans to take care of you, not abandon you, plans to give you the future you hope for" (Jeremiah 29:11). What an awesome promise. Do we believe it? Do we live like we believe it? If not, why not, and can we make today the first day of this journey?

With all the uncertainty in the world today, having someone to rely on that keeps the stars in the sky sounds like a very good option. So, why do we find it so hard to do that on a day-to-day, hour-to-hour basis? Again, we live in a world where knowledge is king, and to have faith and put our trust in someone or something we can't see doesn't make sense. However, we put our trust in things everyday that we can't see. Rather than enumerate those things you, I encourage you to make your own list. I start with vitamin B. Now, you are on your own.

Scripture is filled with examples of people who trusted God in a way very few of us ever have or ever will. Not because we don't want to, but because over time and as society has evolved, we have become less dependent on God and more dependent on ourselves. We trust what we can see and touch: our bank accounts, our friends, our family, and that which requires little to no faith.

To trust means we feel as though we can determine what other people will do, and what might happen in certain situations. If those in our circle can be trusted, then we are safe now and in the future. The only problem with this model is people are not always trustworthy and they will eventually disappoint us. Not because they want to, but because they are human. This is why having a personal, ongoing relationship with the living God, who is not only completely trustworthy, but omnipotent and omniscient, makes enormous sense, especially in today's world. "Trust in the Lord will all your heart and lean not on your own understanding; in all your ways acknowledge Him, and He will make your paths straight" (Proverb 3:5–6).

Again, God is asking us to trust Him but He also makes us a promise. He will make our paths straight.

But, is it just trust? No. It is trust in Him, acknowledging Him in all you do, and not relying on your own abilities. That is not as easy as it sounds. All trust is rooted in the faith that the object of our trust is in fact trustworthy. Scripture says, "It is better to trust in the Lord that to put confidence in princes" (Psalm 118:9). If we have faith in the Lord and believe He is who He says He is, then trusting Him comes easily. If not, we will continue to struggle and fall back on our own abilities and those of the world around us. However, when we are able to trust God, have complete faith in Him, and know He is perfectly capable of doing all the right things for us—what freedom that brings.

Imagine living every day with the complete confidence and knowledge that as you walk with God, listening to and for His voice, your steps will be ordained by God and for God. Your life would be a living example of the phrase, "He walked with God." Furthermore, note this account of faith in Hebrews 11:6. "And, without faith it is impossible to please Him, for whoever would draw near to God must believe that He exists and that He rewards those who seek Him."

Trust is an emotional and complicated issue from our human perspective, which is clearly all we have. This is why we have such difficulty translating our human idea of trust into a Godly form of trust. The truth is without the intervention of God and the Holy Spirit, we are unable to have the faith or trust that is necessary to live the life of Abraham, Ruth, Noah or Joseph in the twenty-first century. Can we do it? Of course. Is it easy? Of course, not. But, as we have all heard while growing up, anything worth having is worth working for, and living the Christ-centered life takes work. It requires work, obedience, knowledge of His word, and desire to grow and to make a difference for Him in this world.

There is a hymn that has been playing in my head throughout this entire chapter, "Trust and Obey." The words speak for themselves.

> When we walk with the Lord
> In the light of His Word,
> What a glory He sheds on our way;
> While we do His good will,
> He abides with us still,
> And with all who will trust and obey.

> Trust and obey,
> For there's no other way
> To be happy in Jesus,
> But to trust and obey.

> Not a shadow can rise,
> Not a cloud in the skies,
> But His smile quickly drives it away;
> Not a doubt or a fear,
> Not a sigh or a tear,
> Can abide while we trust and obey.

> Not a burden we bear,
> Not a sorrow we share,
> But our toil He doth richly repay;

Not a grief or a loss,
Not a frown or a cross,
But is blest if we trust and obey.

But we never can prove
The delights of His love,
Until all on the altar we lay;
For the favor He shows,
And the joy He bestows,
Are for them who will trust and obey.

Then in fellowship sweet
We will sit at His feet,
Or we'll walk by His side in the way;
What He says we will do;
Where He sends, we will go,
Never fear, only trust and obey.

The story of how this song came to be is something we all need to know and understand. This is the simple message of the Gospels, which I found at the website www.sharefaith.com, on March 13, 2015.

In 1887, just following an evangelistic meeting held by Dwight L. Moody, a young man, stood to share his story in an after-service testimony meeting. As he was speaking, it became clear to many that he knew little about the Bible or acceptable Christian doctrine. His closing lines, however, spoke volumes to seasoned and new believers alike: "I'm not quite sure. But, I'm going to trust, and I am going to obey."

So, as we continue our Christian walk, let us keep the

words of scripture and the song on a continuously playing thread in our lives. Let us walk with God, live for Him, and long for more of Him. He wants that, not because He needs it, but because He doesn't. He wants it because He loves us so much that He wants to have the type of relationship all parents want to have with their children. We are His children and He is our Father.

How Does This Work in My Everyday Life?

There are some who will say they trust people until they are given a reason not to trust them. That might work for some. Others trust no one and this comes, for the most part, as a result of being hurt. The truth is the only one truly worthy of our complete trust is God, but, unfortunately, we have to live life here on earth.

To trust, we must be discerning as it relates to people. As we get to know people, we will begin to see whether they are trustworthy or not. Some people can be trusted in some areas, but not others. Trust is built over time, but can be broken overnight.

The best advice I can give regarding how trust works in our everyday lives, is that you should be discerning, allow the Lord to direct your relationships, and, hopefully, then trust will be built.

Trust
Reflection Questions and Advice

1. How important is trust in a relationship? Why?

2. How does one build trust in your relationship with the Lord? And, with others?

3. What are some of the roadblocks to our having a trusting relationship with the Lord?

4. There are several verses in scripture that say those who trust will never be put to shame. What does that mean, and does knowing this make trusting easier? (Check out Romans 10:11; Romans 9:33; and 1 Peter 2:6.)

5. Write in your journal about some of the areas where you find trust difficult. Place those concerns in the hands of God and try to trust a little more each day.

- 7 -

LOVE ONE ANOTHER

"And He has given us this command:
Whoever loves God must also love his brother."
I John 4:21

When I began to think about this chapter and read various possible sources, the very topic of love seemed, at best, overwhelming. Has any subject been written about more than love? How many songs have been written about good love, love gone wrong, love restored, love destroyed…love, love, love. It has become an overused word, and, I am afraid, one that has lost its true meaning in a culture and world where people fall in love, get married, have children (and not necessarily in that order), and then get divorced so easily. Love has become a commodity, handled with little or no care, .

What Is Love?

According to the New Oxford American Dictionary, love is "an intense feeling of deep affection; a deep romantic or sexual attraction to someone." Well, that sort of explains what has happened to our culture. Once the feelings of deep affection or sexual attraction are gone, so is love. So, we move on to our next object of deep affection. Feelings are, in my opinion, neutral. They should not be judged as either right or wrong. They just are. What you do with those feelings may not be neutral. I feel like killing my little sister—this is a feeling. Actually killing my little sister goes well beyond feelings into the sphere of action. There is a difference.

Jesus said the great commandment was, "Love one another. As I have loved you, so you must love one another" (John 13:34). Notice that nowhere do we read that this only applies if you have feelings of love. He also says, in Luke 6, that we are to love our enemies, pray for them, do good to those who hate us, and that there is no glory in loving those who love us. Sinners do that. Love is an action verb and one that was and is personified in the person of Jesus Christ. He is love and we, as His followers, should exhibit the same qualities as Jesus. A baseball glove takes on the shape of its owner, and so should we.

It Is All Greek to Me

There are five Greek words for love. The first is **epithumia**. This word, as used in the Bible, means strong desire, which is a positive connotation, and the negative meaning would be lust. The positive meaning is evoked in Philippians 1:23. This desire has nothing to do with sexual feelings, and everything to do with

Paul's longing to serve the Lord.

The second Greek word for love is **eros**. We all know that this type of love is primarily a passionate love driven by sexual desire. I say primarily because eros could be used for a love that is more than philia love but not sexual in nature. Eros is not used in scripture.

The third Greek word for love is **storge**. This means affection, as between parents and children. This word is not used in scripture, but there are many examples of this type of love: Noah and his family, Naomi and Ruth, and Jacob and his sons.

The fourth Greek word for love is **phillia**. This means friendship, a dispassionate, virtuous love. In The Four Loves, C.S. Lewis differentiates this type of love from the others. Lewis states that friendships, like that between David and Jonathan, have become nearly extinct. This is the type of love that Jesus had for the disciples. This is the type of love we should have for those we are on this journey with.

And the final Greek word for love is **agape**. This type of love is the one most recorded in the New Testament. For example, there is the well-known verse in Matthew 22:39, "Love your neighbor as yourself." Also, note the verse at John 15:12," This is my commandment, that you love one another as I have loved you." Another word used for this type of love is charity. That is the love that allows you to be a caring person regardless of the circumstances.

Love Is a Learned Response

One might think that loving and being loved are as natural as breathing. I submit that they are not. Love is something we all need, and spend extraordinary amounts of time and money seeking. Love has been called that which makes the world go around. Love, in today's culture, comes in many forms, and, unfortunately, they are not all good. The love we read about in the Bible seems to be in very short supply in our world. For example, the love Ruth had for her mother-in-law Naomi. Today, there are cruel jokes made about mothers-in-law, and we have all been guilty of laughing at them. Another example is the love of the mother who sacrifices her child to another woman when Solomon said the baby should be cut in half. I have often said that when you truly love someone, you want God's best for that person, whether or not it includes you. The mother of Moses let him go to save him. The father of Isaac was willing to sacrifice him out of his love of God. Ruth gave up her family, friends, and country for her love of Naomi and Naomi's God. Do we see this type of love today? Do you have any relationships that would encompass any of these types of love?

You can't give away what you don't have, so where do we get the love we need? Where do we get the love that we give to our friends, children, family, and, most importantly, God? We have our first love experience as children. Our parents and siblings are our first love objects. Of course, we don't know it is love. All we know is that we are being fed, cleaned, embraced, touched, talked to, and just generally treated like we are the center of the universe. But, we do reach an age where we equate the way others treat us with love (or not).

In his book, Abba's Child, Brennan Manning states that "the deepest desire of our hearts is for union with God. From the first moment of our existence our most powerful yearning is to fulfill the original purpose of our lives—to see Him more clearly, love Him more dearly, follow Him more nearly." We are made for God, and nothing less will really satisfy us. So, how do we, who so often feel unlovable, enter into the perfect loving relationship with God? And, how do we achieve this with those around us?

If we presume that love is a feeling, we may never reach this place of unconditional obligation. There are many biblical sections that speak of the importance of love. "If you love me you will keep my commandments" (John 14:15). "By this all men will know that you are my disciples, if you love one another" (John 13:35). "But, God demonstrates his own love for us in this: While we were still sinners, Christ died for us" (Romans 5:8).

These three verses show us what God expects from us. He expects us to love Him and obey Him, and to love one another. Also, His sacrificial love for us as shown by His willing death on the cross. Is there anyone in your life for whom you have this type of love? Do you see this type of love among your Christian friends? Do you feel and know Jesus's overwhelming love for you?

How Do We Learn to Love?

Blaise Pascal said: "There is a God-shaped vacuum in the heart of every man which cannot be filled by any created thing, but only by God, the Creator, made known through Jesus." We all have spent countless hours attempting to fill that vacuum with love in the form of food, drugs, alcohol, sex, television, and many other diversions. It doesn't work. As Christians, we know this fact intellectually, but every time we take steps toward a healthy relationship with Jesus, Satan pitches a tent in our minds, convincing us we are not worthy of anyone's love, especially the love our God. We are unworthy. And, we know that if we are told anything often enough, we begin to believe it.

So, in order for us to learn to love—first ourselves and then others—we must accept Jesus's love in the deepest places of our hearts. We not only have to know this truth intellectually, but experientially. We must know in every fiber of our being that it was God's love for us that held Jesus to the cross. If God has this depth of love for us, then why do we have trouble loving ourselves and those around us? Satan plays a huge role in this, I believe. The last thing Satan wants is for us to believe God. So, being the great liar and deceiver, He plants all manner of things in our minds that keep us from getting closer to God. In order for us to rid our minds and hearts of his lies, we must first recognize this, and replace his lies with the love that only God can provide through Jesus.

Easier said than done, but not impossible. Based on the number of Google searches for love, (about 7.6 billion, which is more that the population of the entire earth), I would say that people are curious, desperate, or desirous of experiencing love. But Google is not where we go to find love; we go to the cross, we go to our Lord, and we go to Jesus. Those are our filling stations. Those are our sources of love. Those of us who have a personal relationship with Jesus Christ know the joy, peace, and love found in that relationship. The Bible teaches "God is love" (1John 4:8), and as we walk with Him, we find out that God is not only always there for us, but always loving us, always waiting with open arms to forgive us, and always glad to see us. He is, after all, our Father.

The Blessings of Love

This statement that there are blessings that come with love may seem to be one of those that would get the response," of course there are," from the majority of people. Isn't love the blessing? Yes and no. The God-shaped vacuum could also be referred to as the love-shaped vacuum. If God is love, that would make sense. There are poems written about it, movies made about it, songs written about it, and wars fought over it. It has been described as that which makes the world go 'round.

The blessings start with the loving relationship we have with God. We love our parents, siblings, friends, and children, but that love is conditional no matter what we say. We would all like to think we love unconditionally, and we do, as long as things are going well. The blessings of the love God has for us is that it is unconditional, forgiving, grace-filled, and merciful, no matter what we have done! Is there anything that makes us feel more loved than knowing there is someone in our lives that is as dependable as the sun rising each day? No, but this love cannot be found in a person, but only in that relationship that can truly fill that vacuum in our heart. The blessing is we then have a source of love, and can spread that love to those around us. The blessing is that we have attached ourselves to the greatest source of love in all eternity, and we will never run out as long as we stay attached. The blessing is that all our loneliness and hurt can be wiped away with the loving hand of Jesus. Our responsibility is to give Him that pain and hurt, and He will in turn give you a heart transplant, one that is filled with His love. This is the source of the love He is talking about when He says, "A new command I give you: Love one another. As I have loved you, so you must love one another. All men will know that you are my disciples if you love one another" (John 13:34–35).

It is this love that God gives us, to build us up and to build up and encourage the body of Christ. But, it is also the love that we are to bring to a world in pain. The blessing here is that this love can and will heal the pain. Start with yourself, know and accept His love for you, and then share that love with the hurting world around you.

"Love must be sincere. Hate what is evil; cling to what is good.

Be devoted to one another in brotherly love. Honor one another above yourselves. Never be lacking in zeal, but keep your spiritual fervor, serving the Lord. Be joyful in hope, patient in affliction, faithful in prayer..." (Romans 12:9–12)

How Does This Work in My Everyday Life?

If I truly had an answer to the mystery of love, I would not be writing this book. I would be home counting my money from having sold the information to everyone wanting the answer. Based on the billions of Google searches for the word "love" in all its forms, you can tell that the interest in it is powerful and pervasive.

Love is one of those things we never seem to have enough of, and something we can't give away unless we are having our own supply of love refilled on a regular basis. So, how do we do that? I've made it clear, I hope, that the best and truest source of love is God. He is love—sinless, forgiving, grace-filled and mercy-filled love. He loves us because He is the one who knows us best. But, again, we have to live our life here on earth, often surrounded by unlovable people.

Love is a feeling and an emotion, and not a conscious act of our will. Love is something that our parents model for us, hopefully, and if not then we are going to have struggles with identifying and holding onto true love.

The closest we can come to perfect love is what we feel for our children. But, even that has its limits, and can't truly be called unconditional.

Jesus has asked us to love one another as He has loved us. We can see at John 13:34 that His love for us is what held Him on the cross. I know my love for those in my life is not undying, however I love them in the best way I know how.

The best and only example of love is Jesus, and the manner in which He lived His life here on earth. So, whether or not you had good or bad examples of love, use Him as the one whose example we should follow.

Love One Another

Reflection Questions and Advice

1. Why do you think we have such a hard time loving ourselves?

2. Do you believe that God truly loves you the way He says He does? If not, why not?

3. Can we love others if we don't truly love ourselves?

4. Do you believe you love unconditionally?

5. How can we experience the love God has for us?

- 8 -

HOSPITALITY

"Share with God's people who are in need. Practice hospitality."
Romans 12:13

What Is Hospitality?

According to the New American Oxford Dictionary, hospitality is defined as, "The friendly and generous reception and entertainment of guests, visitors or strangers." In the book of Romans 12:13, we are instructed to, "Share with God's people who are in need. Practice hospitality." Now, I know the first thing that comes to your mind when you hear a verse like this. Some people just don't have the gift of hospitality, and I am one of those people. I have a job, three kids, a husband and barely have time to shower at the end of a day, let alone be hospitable. Well, first of all, this is not a suggestion for a chosen few gifted with a Martha Stewart gene.

Carl Henry, a well-known theologian, says that "Christian hospitality is not a matter of choice, money, age, social standing, sex, or personality. Christian hospitality is a matter of obedience to God." There is that pesky word again, obedience. The one we started the book with, which is the foundation upon which our faith journey is built. So, knowing that we are commanded to be hospitable, how do we go about it? What does it require of us? And, remember, Jesus practiced hospitality and he had no home, no spouse, and no job, and, yet, all He had He shared.

How Do We Learn Hospitality?

The best place in the Bible to seek guidance regarding hospitality is Romans 12. Paul, instructs us to "present our bodies as a living sacrifice to God." What does this mean, how do we do it, and what does it have to do with hospitality?

All those things that we are commanded to do as "acts of obedience" must be the result of a life surrendered to God, totally. If that is the case, all we do will be an outpouring of that surrendered life, and a desire to be obedient and honor God. Paul continues in chapter 12 to command us to "love without hypocrisy, be kind and affectionate with one another and be tender with one another. Be joyful in hope, patient in affliction, and faithful in prayer. Bless those who persecute you, bless and do not curse." Well, that is a pretty tall order for anyone. We all know that one of the main complaints against Christians is that we are hypocrites. Just so we understand, the New Oxford American Dictionary says hypocrisy is "the practice of claiming to have moral standards or beliefs to which one's own behavior does not conform." Telling your children to not smoke or drink when you openly do both is hypocrisy. Have we all been guilty of this? Yes. Do we listen to people who say one thing and do another? Of course, not. So, if we are going to be followers of Christ, then we must not be hypocrites. We must be obedient.

One of my favorite authors, Brennan Manning, said, "The greatest single cause of atheism in the world today is Christians who acknowledge Jesus with their lips and walk out the door and deny Him by their lifestyle. That is what an unbelieving world finds unbelievable." That is a painful statement to read, especially if you believe it and I do. When you go back to the title of this book and combine that thought with Manning's statement, you comprehend the struggle of many Christians. We want to be liked so we don't offend, rock the boat, or color outside the lines. And, as a result we appear to be no different than anyone else.

Author and speaker Nancy Leigh DeMoss did a radio teaching series Revive Our Hearts , about hospitality several years ago, and she gave ten reasons why we need to know and hear about the subject of hospitality.

1. Hospitality is one of the most practical ways to express the love of Christ.
2. That's how people can know that we love them, and that we love each other as believers— through hospitality.

3. Hospitality reflects the hospitable heart of God.
4. We have a God who is hospitable. When we practice hospitality, we show the world what He is like.

5. Hospitality is a great way to build unity and community with others. Being a part of each other's lives does not happen just within the four walls of a church. That's where we meet each other, but then we come into one another's homes and break bread. We also break barriers and create a climate for true fellowship and love to be experienced.
6. The Bible promises rewards for those who practice hospitality.
7. There are some blessings that you'll never experience unless you show hospitality. Those blessings, by the way, are not only here on earth.
8. Hospitality is one of the most effective ways to create a hunger for Christ in the hearts of nonbelievers.
9. Some people who won't go in the door of a church will come into your home. That's where we can begin to share with them the love of Christ.
10. Hospitality will help you deal with loneliness and depression.
11. There are singles and those who are widowed or divorced, who live by themselves and have to deal with loneliness and discouragement for whom showing hospitality is a gift and blessing.
12. Hospitality will help us deal with selfishness.

13. Now, I know most of us have no problem with being selfish. Hospitality is a way of running into the face of that selfishness, and breaking down that natural selfish instinct.
14. Hospitality will help you deal with materialism, and help you develop values that are eternal.
15. In order to be hospitable we will often have to stretch
16. ourselves physically as well as financially.
17. If you have children, hospitality is a great way to cultivate in their hearts a passion for ministry, and a passion for serving other people.
18. Children, like us, are not inclined to think of others first, so we must teach by example.
19. God commands us to be hospitable.
20. If you're a child of God, I have news for you. Hospitality is not an option; it is a commandment.

A life surrendered to God will be one in which He guides us through our Christian journey. It will be that which creates in us a clean heart and a desire to obey God and follow His teachings. Consider Romans 12.:13 "Share with God's people who are in need. Practice hospitality." And, practice makes perfect. Just in case any men reading this book think that the hospitality issue is for women only, we see in I Timothy 1:2 and Titus 1:8 that one of the requirements of being a leader, elder, teacher, or deacon in the church is the virtue of hospitality.

This, again, is not something we do only if time, money, and energy allow. This is not something that we do when we feel like it. My children used to say, "I don't want to get up." I would reply, "Jesus didn't want to die, but He did, so get up." Hospitality is something we should pray about, prepare for, and welcome as opportunities for it come our way.

Over nearly forty years of marriage, my husband and I have taken quite a few people into our home. Most were pregnant girls with no place to live. They wanted to carry their babies to term with no one to help. So we became those people. We have taken in young men out of jail who also had nowhere to turn, and we have also taken in families who were struggling and needed a safe place to heal. Often, people would look at us as though we weren't playing with a full deck, but never once did we feel as though we were not blessed more for having shown hospitality. The blessing of being obedient is most often to be blessed. Our life is richer and fuller for having been obedient.

Now, in 1 Peter 4, my heading says, "Living for God." In verse 7 Peter says, "Above all, love each other deeply, because love covers a multitude of sins. Offer hospitality to one another, without grumbling." That means you must offer it with a generous, willing heart without complaint, as if Jesus was our guest. He is the empty chair at every table.

These are things we are commanded to do. I think a recurrent theme in each of these chapters is that these topics are not suggestions made by God, but they are commandments. We often don't see them that way, maybe because of the way they are written. Of course, if Moses goes to a mountaintop and writes the Ten Commandments in stone, we will definitely pay attention. But when Paul tells us to practice hospitality, it doesn't have the same urgency and authority. But, they are no less important. My ten topics are just a few of the New Testament commandments, which form the basis of who we are as Christians. It is what the world sees when they look at us. And, trust me, they are looking. If we are going to call ourselves followers of Christ, then hospitality must be one of the tools in our toolbox.

I am sure most of us look at these commandments from Jesus, and prioritize some as more important than others. We think not committing adultery is more important to the Lord than being hospitable. I can't say that thinking is true or not true, but I have learned one thing in my forty-eight-year journey with the Lord. If He cared enough to put it in the Bible, it is important! How important? We have all heard the story of Sodom and Gomorrah, even those who have never read the Bible. We know that these two cities were destroyed by God because of the lawlessness and depravity that was allowed to flourish there. But, in Ezekiel 16:48–50, God puts forth another reason.

Now this was the sin of your sister Sodom: She and her daughters were arrogant, overfed and unconcerned; they did not help the poor and needy. They were haughty and did detestable things before me. Therefore I did away with them as you have seen.,

Well, that is clear. They did not help the poor, they

were without compassion, and they were haughty. And, as a result of those things they were done away with!

As Christians, we are told that we are the hands and feet of Jesus, and that we may be the only Jesus someone ever sees. If you believe that, and I do, then every word and act should be held captive by His will and in obedience to Him.

In I Timothy 5:9–10, we are told that in order for a widow of the church to receive help from the church, she must qualify by being sixty years old, faithful to her husband, and well known for her good deeds, which would include hospitality. Again, hospitality is something that is expected from all Christians.

Blessings of Hospitality

As I stated earlier, on those occasions where we practiced hospitality, we were the ones who were blessed. Our circle became richer and larger, and our hearts were filled. In 3 John 5–8, John writes to Gaius and thanks him for the hospitality he has shown those disciples who were travelling around spreading the Gospel.

"You do well to send them on their way in a manner worthy of God. It was for the sake of the Name that they went out, receiving no help from the pagans. We ought therefore to show hospitality to such men so that we may work together for the truth."

As Christians we have a responsibility to provide whatever we are called to provide for those who have been called to spread the Gospel. And, we also, as Christians, should be aware of all those around us who may be strangers in need. "Keep on loving each other as brothers. Do not forget to entertain strangers, for by so doing some have entertained angels without knowing it" (Hebrews 13:1–2).

It would be an amazing blessing to entertain an angel, but unless we are obedient to the teaching, chances are pretty slim. Samuel Johnson, the poet, essayist, and writer said, "The true measure of a man is how he treats someone who can do him absolutely no good." That should be the measure of a Christian, especially in light of our example. Jesus, a sinless man, died a gruesome death for the sins of all, many of whom will never acknowledge Him. That is the ultimate sacrifice for those who can do nothing for Him. God doesn't need us; He wants us. God created us for His pleasure, and wants nothing more than to love us and be loved in return. It seems so simple when you read it, but not so to do it. Jesus is also our example of hospitality and he was a homeless man, living alone in the desert with a rather full schedule, preparing to save all mankind. So, the next time you feel like you just can't open your heart or door to one more person, look up and remember Jesus's example.

Opening our lives in a hospitable way will reap such incredible blessings for those of us willing to do it, not the least of which is knowing we are being obedient to our Lord and Savior. And as C.S. Lewis said:

"Friendship is unnecessary, like philosophy, like art…It has no survival value; rather it is one of those things that give value to survival. Hospitality is friendship in action."

How Does This Work in My Everyday Life?

How can we all be more hospitable? This is the one obligation many prefer to overlook by saying it is not their calling or gift. "I only have a small apartment, I'm a single man, too many kids." All of that may be true, but you can still be hospitable. Jesus was a single man, without a home, paying job, and had twelve ragtag buddies who followed Him around. We are not being asked to feed the masses and house homeless people, but we are being asked to share whatever the Lord has blessed us with. That may be money, food, shelter, or whatever else someone may need. It may be a shoulder to cry on, gas for someone's car, or whatever. We must be willing to be hospitable with whomever the Lord brings our way. And, again, like so many other things, it must be a conscious act of our wills.

Practice Hospitality
Reflection Questions and Advice

1. How do you practice hospitality?

2. Did hospitality play any part for you coming to know the Lord?

3. Read Luke 14:12–14. Is this something you would do or maybe have done? If yes, why and what was the result?

4. In Proverbs 31:20, the woman is described as one who opens her arms to the poor and her hands to the needy. Are you that person, and if not, what do you plan to do to change that?

5. Each day try to find one simple act of hospitality that you can offer someone. Remember, hospitality is not just opening your home, but your heart, and making people feel loved. It is being Jesus to a hurting world.

- 9 -

PURITY

"Blessed are the pure in heart for they shall see God."
Matthew 5:8

This book has been in the making, both in my head and on paper, for what seems like forever. There have been many starts and stops, but as I come down the home stretch, the Lord is still driving the car and changing plans. My original chapter 9 was entitled Accountability. But for whatever reason, which I believe the Lord will reveal, it is now entitled Purity. Not sure why, but it makes sense.

What Is Purity?

So, I begin as I have the other topics and head to my trusty New Oxford American Dictionary. "Purity...free from adulteration or contamination; Freedom from immorality, especially of a sexual nature; white is meant to represent purity and innocence."

Purity is not only a word that we hear very little of in today's culture, but when we do, it usually has to do with laundry soap, food we eat, or the driven snow. The question is why that is the case, and is it different among professing Christians? If you were to ask Christians what purity is, many would probably go to Matthew 5:8: "blessed are the pure in heart for they shall see God." But what does it mean to be pure in heart?

I believe it can be safely said that the concept of purity is a thing of the past. I am not even sure if the average young person would understand the meaning of the word as it relates to them. An example of this would be the book by Jessica Valenti, The Purity Myth: How America's Obsession with Virginity is Hurting Young Women. So, here we see that purity is a hurtful myth. The operative word in that sentence is myth.

In America today, purity is nearly always thought of with a sexual connotation. But, as Christians, purity takes on a much bigger meaning. We should have different goals and desires than secular society. We need to ask ourselves, "What is it we are living for, and what do we desire the most?" A beatitude answers these questions clearly. "Blessed are the pure in heart, for they shall see God."

Purity—in all ways—should be our desire so that we can see God. Sounds simple, but it is very difficult. If you look closely at the other beatitudes, you will see that a pure heart is necessary.

Purity was first used in the Bible to mean the opposite of unclean, extending to animals, food, or people. Anything that God deemed unclean was to be avoided. However, if you look closely you will see that things God once called unclean were made clean. Why? The arbitrary decisions God makes, I believe, are necessary to make sure we realize He is God and sovereign, and wants our obedience.

How Can We Be Pure?

We tend to be more concerned with looking pure outwardly, but in Deuteronomy 10:16, Moses said, "Circumcise your hearts, therefore, and do not be stiff-necked any longer." And, Samuel asked Saul in I Samuel 15:22, "Does the Lord delight in burnt offerings and sacrifices and much as obeying the Lord? To obey is better than sacrifice and to heed is better than the fat of rams." Here, we see that the heart of the matter is the matter of the heart.

To be pure begins with an attitude of the heart. It means having a heart that is totally committed to living a life that is sold out to God. It means every thought, word and, deed is held captive in a pure heart that desires to please and serve the Lord. Can this be done? Not without divine intervention. In Jeremiah 17:9, God says: "The heart is hopelessly dark and deceitful, a puzzle that no one can figure out. But, I, God, search the heart and examine the mind. I get to the heart of the human. I get to the root of things. I treat them as they really are, not as they pretend to be."

So, just to make sure we all understand, purity is only possible with the help of God. We, as humans, are not capable of any sort of permanent purity without God's help. And, the key to that help is for us to acknowledge we need it and ask for it. We do need, however, to ask for the right reason. "When you ask you do not receive, because you ask with the wrong motives, that you may spend what you get on your pleasures" (James 4:3).

How many of us have thought of what we would do if we won the lottery? Houses, cars, trips, jewelry, and if there is anything left, tithe to the Lord. Our thought and heart are set on our own pleasures, and not those of serving and obeying the Lord.

I had a good friend who was what we refer to as a godly woman. She was seen this way by all who knew her. One day, I asked her if she had ever really done anything horrible. She told me that as a child she had picked up a piece of gum from the floor and had eaten it. Gum was not allowed in her family. All I could think was, "Oh the horror! Really, that's the best you've got?" She followed that up, however, with the following thought. She said while she had never struggled with alcohol, drugs, or sexual promiscuity, the sins in her heart that only God knew of were far more dangerous. If you are a fall-down drunk, sooner or later people notice, but if your harbor bitterness, jealousy, or hate in your heart, know that "the Lord searches every heart and understands every motive behind the thoughts" (I Chronicles 28:9).

So, again, the purity we seek must begin in our hearts. There are natural or physical laws and when some are broken, there are consequences. If you put your hand in fire you get burned. But, Daniel did not get burned because God can override physical laws. We can't. Miracles cannot be explained by natural law, rather a gift from God.

God has given us moral laws which even He cannot break. He cannot lie, cheat, or steal, but He can and does hold us responsible when we break His morals laws. Physical laws generally have immediate consequences—moral laws not always—but there are consequences. And, having a pure heart means that we keep God's moral laws. We tend to think of sexual impurity more than other forms of impurity. In the book of Hosea, we see what happens when a people, and in this case Israel, throw purity to the wind and feed their lusts of all types. God deals harshly with them, not just because of their behavior, but because there seemed to be no desire to please or serve God. This is spiritual adultery. We commit spiritual adultery every time we stray off the path God has designed for us. Notice I said the path God has designed, not the path we have designed. Purity desires to follow and please God every step of the way.

How Do We Have a Pure Heart?

We have already said that apart from divine intervention, we are unable to have a pure heart. We have seen that the heart of man is wicked above all things. We have all heard people say that, "People are fundamentally good." If this is true, who teaches you to lie, cheat, steal, and say hurtful things? No one does. We are born knowing how to do these things because of the deceitfulness in our hearts. The Russian novelist Ivan Turgenev said, "I do not know what the heart of a bad man is like, but I do know what the heart of a good man is like, and it is terrible." And, that is assuming there are any good men.

In the book of Hebrews 10:24, we are encouraged to, "Let us consider how we can spur one another on toward love and good deeds." We need to train our hearts to do what is good, pure, and right, and we need each other for the encouragement to move forward.

The whole purpose of this book is to challenge each other to actually live our lives in such a way as to stand out and up for Jesus. To live our lives so that others will look at us and say, "Boy are they different," and have that difference be not only good, but something that attracts other to Christ. If people who know you don't recognize you and your lifestyle as being Christian, maybe we need to sift our words, thoughts, and deeds through a stronger filter. Filter out the impurities. We need to examine our inner life, and see where we need to change. We need to examine our motivations, the atmosphere around us, how we talk to and about people and how can I work toward a purity of heart and show God's love to those in my life. We need to take Philippians 4:8 and have it inscribed into our hearts. "Whatever is true, whatever is noble, whatever is right, whatever is pure, whatever is lovely, whatever is admirable—if anything is excellent or praiseworthy—think about such things."

Blessings of Purity

In Matthew 5:8, we are given a promise for living a pure life. We will see God. Now, we know that when we accept Christ as our Savior and turn our life over to Him, we are promised eternal life with Him in heaven. But, what about before we get to heaven? Can we see Him on this side? I don't believe we can see God, but we are certainly able to see the evidence of Him.

I believe the main blessing of living a life of purity is that it is pleasing to God. All that we do and say needs to come from a heart and life surrendered to God. We need to take the Philippians verse and use it as a yardstick by which we measure our walk with the Lord. However, in order to be able to recognize noble, right, and admirable, we need to know God, know scripture, and know what God wants and expects from us as Christians. Most of us have a fairly good idea of what He doesn't want from us, which is a good place to start, but we need to know Him and His heart so well that His words abide in us and the actions follow.

As stated at the beginning of this chapter, purity is a word that isn't used a great deal in today's culture. Aside from the food we eat and detergent we use, purity seems to be a thing of the past. How did we, as Christians, allow this to happen, and what are we doing about it? From where I sit, we're doing very little to nothing. Christian youth live together before marriage, have babies out of wedlock, get divorced at the same rate as non-Christians, abuse drugs and alcohol, and the list goes on. A former pastor said to me recently, "If being a Christian were a crime, would there be enough evidence to convict you?" Purity is only one of the myriad ways that we stand out, but does your life resemble the life of Christ closely enough for others to see Him in you? Are you God with skin on in your world? Are you the hands and feet of Jesus? We read in I Peter 4:2 what we should, as followers of Christ, strive for: "he does not live the rest of his earthly life for evil human desires, but rather for the will of God."

So, as we continue our walk with the Lord, we need to embrace our hearts and minds, and hold them captive to the will of God. We do this by reading and memorizing scripture, through fellowship with believers, prayer, and most of all by seeking and following the will of God. Keep our eyes on Him, keep our hearts filled with His word, and surrender your desires to His desires for us. This is not a one-time event, but a daily and lifelong quest, but hopefully with God's help and guidance each small step will be forward toward the reward.

How Does This Work in My Everyday Life?

So, being pure is not unlike being holy in terms of our inability to achieve a pure heart. Purity is a state that can only be achieved with the help of God, and then it will only be a temporary condition. Purity aims at the most perfect of all things. We are not perfect, but with Jesus as our role model, we can move in the direction of being pure. Like other virtues of Jesus we wish to attain, knowing and following his teaching in scripture is the path we need to follow.

Purity

Reflection Questions and Advice

1. How can you effect change in the attitude our culture has toward purity?

2. In what area of your life do you have the biggest struggle with purity?

3. What can you do to combat this problem? Are you doing it?

4. Is it realistic to think we can be pure? Why, or why not?

5. How can we seek God with a pure heart and mind?

- 10 -

CARE FOR WIDOWS AND ORPHANS

"Religion that God our father accepts as pure and faultless is this: to look after orphans and widows in their distress and to keep oneself from being polluted by the world."
James 1:27

As I was explaining to a friend what I was trying to accomplish with this book, he said that he hoped I would include the commandment articulated in James 1:27: "Religion that God our Father accepts as pure and faultless is this: to look after the orphans and widows in their distress and to keep oneself from being polluted by the world." I am somewhat embarrassed to admit that it was not one of the ones I had chosen. And, it should have been given my passion for adoption, unmarried women with children, and widows. When I examined why I had not thought of this commandment, I realized that there are so many in the New Testament that I needed to limit the book to those that I felt offered us the greatest potential for wholeness and maturing as Christians. My choices were not random, but they were selected for their impact on the greatest number of Christians. And, it is for this reason that including this commandment became critical.

What Is an Orphan?

Again, I go to the New Oxford American Dictionary. An orphan is "a child whose parents are dead; a person or thing bereft of protection." A widow is "a woman whose husband has died and she has not remarried."

I would like to include in this definition of an orphan my personal feeling that we need to care for the children with only one parent as well, which is usually a single mother. We need to step up to the plate and help these women, and if they have sons, and there is no man present in their lives, we need to have a man step in as a role model. If we say we are pro-life, and a young girl has her baby, we need to be there when she needs a break. We need to provide the mother and children with the love and protection of the church and Christ.

God also mandates that we care for orphans. In Jeremiah 22:16, He says, "He defended the cause of the poor and needy, and so all went well. Is that not what it means to know me?" He also says in Jeremiah 49:11, "Leave your orphans; I will protect their lives. Your widows, too, can trust in me."

In today's culture we have many children who are not technically orphans, but they have only one parent, and as I stated earlier, that is usually a single mother. Of course, we have single fathers as well, but in either case what do we do in service to these children?

In 2012, 64 percent of children up to the age of seventeen live with married parents. This is down from 77 percent in 1980. Twenty-four percent of children live with only a mother, while 4 percent live with only fathers, and 4 percent live with neither. Nearly one-third of the child population could be classified as an orphan. Legally, an orphan is a child with only one parent present. According to the US Census Bureau, 120,000 children are parentless, and 400,000 are without permanent families. There is a pool of over a half a million children that need permanent homes, love, and a stable family. So, why do we go to China and Africa to adopt when we have needs right here?

A friend once said to me that if every Evangelical church in the country were to adopt just one child, there would be little need for foster care and nearly every child would have a permanent home. This doesn't seem to be such a huge task, and, after all, this is what God says is pure religion. He does say to "visit the widows and orphans," but I would hope, as followers of Christ, we could go the extra mile and do more than visit.

What Is a Widow?

In the Old Testament, there are very specific laws regarding the treatment of widows. The brother of the dead husband was supposed to marry the widow and keep the bloodline in the family. If the brother did not wish to marry his brother's widow, he was not looked upon favorably by the elders (Deut. 25:5–10).

One of the best-known stories about a widow is the story of Ruth. She not only lost her husband, but her two sons as well. She had two daughters-in-law, Naomi and Orpah. God used her widowhood and Naomi's love for her to create the genealogy of Jesus Christ. From a poor widow, childless daughter-in-law, and Boaz comes the father of Jesse who was the father of David…and so on. God takes a very strong stand throughout scripture on the treatment of widows. In the book of Malachi 3:5, God says He will swiftly judge "sorcerers, adulterers, those who swear falsely, those who oppress the hired worker in his wages, the widow and the fatherless, and those who do not fear me." That certainly gives us a clear idea of how serious God is about caring for widows and orphans.

We have all heard the story of Sodom and Gomorrah, and how God destroyed them because of their sinfulness. A friend of mine who is a respected theologian said that the reason for their destruction was their lack of hospitality and the attitude of their heart. In Ezekiel 16:18, God says, "Behold, this was the guilt of your sister Sodom: she and her daughters had pride, excess of food, and prosperous ease, but did not aid the poor and needy." There is no mention specifically of sexual immorality; however, we can be sure it existed. But, it is clearly stated that they did not aid to poor and the needy. Historically, widows and orphans were referred to as poor and needy. Again,

God lets us know how important these people are to Him, and how important He wants them to be to us. What are you doing to honor His wishes?

One thing I learned very early on as a Christian was that all God wants from us is that we love Him, obey Him, and that we "let our hearts be broken by the things that break the heart of God." This is a quote from Bob Pierce, the founder of Samaritan's Purse and World Vision. Both of these organizations meet the needs of millions of needy and poor around the world, including in this country. They are putting feet on the commandment to care for widows and orphans.

Blessings of Caring for Widows and Orphans

As is the case with all acts of obedience to what God is telling us to do is the knowledge that we are pleasing Him. As a child, I was not the most compliant and obedient. Those who know me would find this to be a gross understatement, but nevertheless true. But, in spite of it, I deeply loved my father, and so much wanted his approval and love back. It was always clear to me when I wasn't pleasing him, but when I was the joy I felt was beyond measure. This is all our Heavenly Father asks. "If you love me you will obey my commandments" (John 14:15). There is no greater blessing than knowing and feeling the love of God, of knowing we are His, and that we are the recipients of His unconditional love.

Be Ye Doers...Blessings

In James 1: 22–25, we are told to not be merely listeners but doers of the word. As much as I love studying the Bible, after being a Christian for forty-eight years, I think I have a pretty good handle on the fundamentals. At times, I want to say—no scream— "okay folks, let's get up and do what the Bible tell us to do." After all, isn't that the point of knowing it? The point is to become the hands and feet of Jesus, God with skin on. To this I say, "yes!"

A friend of mine who is the single mom of two young adults recently told me she went to several churches for help. She wanted to find a man who could mentor her teenage son. She was given a litany of excuses, instead of enthusiastic promises to help. In Matthew 19:14, he says, "Let the little children come to me and do not hinder them, for the kingdom of heaven belongs to such as these."

Because of the dramatic shift in the culture of our country, we have a whole new category of widows and orphans. We have single, never-married women having children without the benefit or desire for a father. So are they widows? No. They have consciously chosen to become parents without a participating father, but that does not mean we should ignore them. Widows and orphans do not choose their status either, but we seem to have more compassion for them than those who knowingly walk into it. Again, we need to remember the example we are to be following. In the book of John 4, Jesus encounters a Samaritan women at a well. Given his culture at the time, He should not have even talked to her, but He not only talked to her but He asked her to draw Him water. Again, this would be an act that the culture would not like. When He confronted her about her five husbands and the fact she was living with a man she was not married to, she knew who He was. As a result of her witness, many Samaritans came to know Christ. Would a woman with this background feel welcome in your home or church? She should.

While we feed the hungry around the world, dig wells for clean water, and build homes for the homeless, we have people living in our own neighborhoods who are just as needy. I am not saying we should not dig wells and feed the hungry. I am saying that we need to look up, reach out, and be ye doers of the word. We can't all travel the world making a difference for Christ, but we can travel our neighborhoods and towns to make a difference.

As we look at the life of Christ, we see that all recorded history is divided into the period before His birth and after His birth. It is something we know, but do we realize the significance of that? Christ is the example we have chosen for our lives. We must take what He says seriously, and that means we must care for the widows, orphans, and anyone else God brings across our path. We must understand His teachings, and we must make every effort possible to make them not just a part of our life, but our life. The last part of the verse says, we are not to be "polluted by the world." We are to be in the world but not of the world. We are to be a light in the darkness. We are to be salty enough to make others thirsty. All of this and more comes out of our desire to put the Lord first in our lives, and to serve Him by serving others.

What Can We Do?

With the prevalence of single parents and widows in our culture, we have many opportunities to serve the Lord. Most of us probably have friends who are single mothers. Most of us know at least one widow, maybe even in our own family. When was the last time you gave that mother a break and took her child for the day? When was the last time you picked up the phone a called a widow you know just to see if there is anything you could do for her.

I know from my own experience how much it means to someone when you reach out just to say "hi." We, as Christians, were meant for community, and that includes widows, orphans, single moms or dads, and anyone else God puts in our life. Know that God has them there for a reason.

Boys who have no father present in their lives are often overlooked. Some churches have shepherding programs in which adult men spend time with boys who have no male present in their home. It is sort of a Christian Boys Club. Rather than list a long line of statistics, suffice it is to say that coming from a fatherless home increases the risk for a multitude of problems for the child. I will cite some particularly egregious statistics. Over 30 percent of white babies are born out of wedlock, while 72 percent of black babies and 50 percent Hispanic are as well. Enough said. So, we have our work cut out for us. As for widows and widowers, we have 8.7 million widows and 2.1 million widowers. The widows make up 40 percent of senior citizens, according to the 2010 Census Bureau statistics. Another way we can be the hands and feet of Jesus would be to visit nursing homes and visit people who don't normally receive visitors on a regular basis. You say you don't have time, but you might be in a nursing home one day wishing someone would visit. Watch the movie Fried Green Tomatoes. It will encourage you.

Care for the Widows and Orphans
Reflection Questions and Advice

1. Make a concrete plan regarding how, when, and where you are going to be the hands and feet of Jesus in the life of a widow, orphan, or single parent.

2. Why do you think this mandate by Jesus is referred to as "pure religion"?

3. Look up the four biblical references to widows and orphans. How are they portrayed in the Bible?

    *   Psalm 82:3

    *   Psalm 10:17

    *   Jeremiah 22:16

    *   Psalm 68:5

4. Does your church have any special programs for single parents, widows, or widowers? If not, is there something you could do?

5. What would you change about the book as a whole? How can it be better? What do I need to address that I didn't?

EPILOGUE

Well, we have come to the end of the ten commandments I chose for this book. I covered a variety of topics, from obedience to purity. As stated in the first chapter of the book, if we aren't willing to make the commitment and decision to be obedient to God's word, none of the rest of the chapters are necessary. My prayer for those of you who have read the book is that you were enriched and challenged by the content. I pray you learned and laughed in the process. The journey we call Christianity is fraught with pitfalls and speed bumps. It can be a journey of glory to glory and bliss to bliss, or it can be like pushing a rope uphill or nailing Jello to the wall. The thing we need to focus on is that in either situation we are accompanied by our Lord and Savior Jesus Christ, who makes all things possible.

We not only need to take the words of Jesus seriously, but we need to put that which we know to be true into action, and, as they say at Nike: just do it!

We need to be doers of the word and not hearers only, and we need to be in the world, but not of the world. And, we need to make a difference wherever we are. And, most importantly, we must exchange the need to be liked for the desire to be obedient to the God who died for us and loves us unconditionally.

I have learned a lot while writing this book, especially about myself and my world. Still, I would love to hear from you. Tell me how this book ministered to you and how it could be better, and anything else you want to tell me. Thank you in advance. Be blessed.

BIBLIOGRAPHY

Cho, Paul Y., *Prayer: The Key to Revival*. [Dallas: Word, 1984] p 48

Stott, John. *Involvement: Being a Responsible Christian in a Non-Christian Society*. [New Jersey: Revell, 1984] p 38

Dawkins, Richard. *The God Delusion*. [New York: Houghton Mifflin 2006] p 7

Worthington, Everett. *Five Steps to Forgiveness*. [New York: Crown 2001] p 22

Yancey, Philip. *Prayer Does It Make a Difference*. [Grand Rapids: Zondervan 2006] p 46

Tikekar, S.R., *Compilation of quotes by Mahatma Gandhi* [www.mkgandhi.org] Volume 7. p 20, 46

Hybels, Bill. *Too Busy Not to Pray*, [Downers Grove, IL: InterVarsity 1998] p 50

Omartian, Stormie. *The Prayer that Changes Everything*. [Eugene, OR: Harvest House 2004] p 51

Lewis, C.S. *Four Loves*. [New York: Houghton Mifflin 1971] p 66

Manning, Brennan, Abba's Child [Colorado Springs: NavPress, 1994] p 67, 74

Converse, Charles c. *What a Friend We Have in Jesus*. Indestructible Phonographic Record Co., 1908. CD. p 51

Towner, D. B. *Trust and Obey*. Edison Blue Amberol, 1914. CD. p 61

ACKNOWLEDGEMENTS

At the risk of forgetting someone, please know that every person whose life has touched mine is responsible for who I am today and therefore the content of this book.

I'd like to thank Shannon Myers and Kristin Kane Ford for taking a chance on me and this book. You have made the journey enjoyable, verging on fun. Thank you Todd Bauders of Contrast Photography for making me look good and for your incredible patience and good humor.

To all who took the time to read the manuscript and either comment or endorse, you are all a blessing. Those whose endorsements you see, please visit their websites. You'll find a link to each one on mine. www.saradormon.com

And especially to the good Lord for His love, patience, grace mercy and marvelous sense of humor.

I love you all.

Sara Dormon

Todd Bauders, Contrast Photography

ABOUT THE AUTHOR

Sara R. Dormon is an author, counselor, mother, advocate and Christian. She is known to tell it like it is and in her most recent book, "If You're a Christian and Everybody Likes You... Something's Wrong" she offers readers a self-reflective journey on what it means to be a Christian in today's society. Sara is also the co-author of the book, "I'm Pregnant...Now What?" and "So You want to Adopt...Now What?" written with Ruth Graham and published by Regal Books.

As an experienced and humorous speaker, Sara brings a refreshing and honest look at some very difficult issues from Christianity to adoption. She has been a speaker for the Ruth Graham & Friends ministry and has also spoken for pro-life, church groups and women's organizations. Sara has served on the board of Amnion Crisis Pregnancy Center, Ruth Graham and Friends Ministry and is currently on the board of Hope Pregnancy Center in Philadelphia.

She is the mother of three sons and the grandmother to four girls and two boys. She lives in a suburb of Philadelphia with her husband Bill.

CPSIA information can be obtained
at www.ICGtesting.com
Printed in the USA
FSOW04n1016121116
27303FS